THE JOY OF DEPRESSION

by

DAVID RUDNITSKY, M.D.*

* Manic Depressive

Illustrated by Jack Medoff

Shapolsky Publishers
New York

For additional information, contact:
Shapolsky Publishers, Inc.
136 West 22nd Street, New York, NY 10011
212/633-2022
FAX 212/633-2123

First Edition 1990

9 8 7 6 5 4 3 2 1

Library of Congress Cataloging-in-Publication Data

Rudnitsky, David A.
The joy of depression / by David Rudnitsky. -- 1st ed.
p. cm.

ISBN: 0-944007-53-8

1. Self-care, Health--Humor. 2. Depression, Mental--Humor.
3. Life style--Humor.

I. Title.

PN6231.S489R83 1989   818'.5407--dc20   89-10752 CIP

Manufactured in the United States of America

DEDICATION

To all my friends, relatives
and associates, without whose
assistance and support,
this book would have been
finished nine years ago.

OTHER BOOKS BY THE AUTHOR

1001 WAYS YOU REVEAL YOUR PERSONALITY*

1001 *MORE* WAYS YOU REVEAL YOUR PERSONALITY*

LOVE CODES*

HOW TO MULTIPLY WITHOUT DIVIDING*

MEN WHO HATE THEMSELVES (AND THE WOMEN WHO AGREE WITH THEM)

*Co-authored with Elayne Kahn, Ph.D.

DISCREDITS

Obviously, the wrath of all civilized people should be directed at my agent Frank Weimann who found the original editor for this - Caleb Mason. After them, all outrage should be directed towards Ian Shapolsky, who picked up where the original publisher left off, after the author told them where *they* could get off.

Of course, no handbook of depression can be complete without those who are most responsible for depressing the author: To Elayne Kahn, who depresses me evertime she says, "That's *Dr*. Elayne Kahn." To Barry Shapiro, who depresses me because *he* married Genevieve Davis. To Erica Ress, who depresses me not only because she's beautiful and rich, but because she also writes better than I do (OK, only slightly).

To Ray Leslie, who depresses me because he's talented and poor, but still gets all those gorgeous dancers. To Lynn Bregman, who depresses me because she moved out of Santa Monica, which means I can't have breakfast at "The Rose" anymore. To Paulette Cooper, who depresses me when she reminds me that she's been *listening* to this stupid book fot the past twelve years. To Abigail Wright, who depresses me with her eclectic knowledge, warmth and sensitivity. To Annie Cohen, who depresses me whenever she mentions how great the UJA benefit party was at the Waldorf, which I missed.

To Sheila Rae, who depresses me with her unbelievable house in the country; To Selma Prezant, who depresses me everytime I think of all the milk she *forced* me to drink. To Lillian Levitt, who depresses me because she still gets a better tan than I do. To Bruce Berger, who depresses me with all those exotic trips to only God Knows Where.

To Steve Hans, who depresses me with his Mercedes, his penthouse, his club: Conscious Point, etc. To Crystal Wu, who depresses me with her style, sense of humor, and beauty; To Steve Klaussner and Janet Fishman, who depress me because they actually *sold* a screenplay and didn't have to split the money. To Gary McKee, who depresses me by being tall, blond, as well as a sensational artist. To Nancy Kitchen, who depresses me just by being so classy. To Michelle de Muth, who depresses me because she was *only* four years old when Sgt. Pepper's came out.

To Louis Lanzano, who's been depressing me for the past twenty years by constantly repeating how great things were in 1965; To Stan Becker, who depressed me by giving me my first advertising job instead of kicking me out of the office, which is what he should have done. To Cara Hetson, who depresses me because she can swim like a fish, cook like a gourmet, and pass for being *extremely* European. To Elyss Emmer, who depresses me whenever she mentions all the lunches that I owe her. To Mary Sorrentino, who depresses me because she was so gracious about getting me the Fax of the cover.

To Phil White, who depresses me because even I can't get a word in edgewise with him. To Larry Leslie (alias Uncle Libby), who depresses me for reasons it would take a book to explain. To Helen Uffner, who depresses me the one day a year that she *doesn't* celebrate her birthday. To Sasha Plutno, who depressed me by moving to Florida. To Helen Lynch, who depresses me just by being located in fabulous Sausilito. To Deanna Estreich, who depresses me by making me realize that craziness really is hereditary in my family.

And finally, to my parents, Sam and Mollie Rudnitsky, who depress me because, *no matter what I do,* they continue to remain optimistic.

TABLE OF CONTENTS

CHAPTERS	PAGE
1. INTRODUCTION: OVERCOMING THOSE TERRIBLE FEELINGS OF OPTIMISM	13
2. DETERMINING YOUR AQ (APATHY QUOTIENT)	17
3 YOUR HORROR SCOPE	25
4. GREAT MOMENTS IN DEPRESSION	37
5. THE LOW SUGAR/HIGH VALIUM DIET	41
6. YOGA FOR DEPRESSION	47
7. THE SENSUOUS CATATONIC	59
8. WHAT COLOR IS YOUR PARANOIA?	65
9. EUROPE ON FIVE LIBRIUM A DAY	73
10. THE NATIONAL ENEMA (VOLUME I)	79
11. YOUR DEPRESSING HIT PARADE	81
12. BELIEVE IT OR NOT OF DEPRESSION	85
13. ANOREXIA: A GREAT WAY TO SLIM DOWN	97
14. THE MOST DEPRESSING TV COMMERCIALS	103
15. THE GREAT DEPRESSION: 1929-30	109
16. SLOUCHING, SLUMPING AND DROOPING	113
17. CHAIN-SMOKING, OBESITY, AND THE GOOD LIFE	121
18. MONOTONY: THE BORED GAME FOR THE WHOLE FAMILY	127

19. THE NATIONAL ENEMA (VOLUME II)   129

20. ANTIDEPRESSENTS: THE COMPLETE
      LOWDOWN   131

21. MOROSE THE CAT (DEPRESSED
      PET OF THE YEAR)   135

22. HOW TO LOSE MONEY DURING
      THE COMING GOOD YEARS   137

23. THE DEPRESSED READING LIST   143

24. DEPRESSIONS IN THE EARTH   147

25. THE NATIONAL ENEMA (VOLUME III)   149

26. DARKNESS, DINGINESS AND OTHER
      DECORATING TIPS   151

27. DRESSING FOR DEPRESSION (OR THE
      SCHLEPPIE HANDBOOK)   157

28. JACK MEDOFF'S REAL-LIFE DEPRESSION   161

29. THE THRILL OF DEFEAT
      (AND THE AGONY OF VICTORY)   167

30. STAYING IN BED:
      THE BEST EXERCISE   173

31. EARNING YOUR D.D.
      (DOCTORATE OF DEPRESSION)   177

1. INTRODUCTION: OVERCOMING THOSE TERRIBLE FEELINGS OF OPTIMISM

Depression is much more than a state of mind — it's a total way of living!

"Why fight it?" That's what millions of Americans and people around the world are saying. Those, much like yourself, who are sick of trying to find a so-called "meaningful" existence. Teachers, doctors, dentists, arsonists and lawyers have all discovered that depression is the perfect way of coping with the stresses and strains of modern life—and it's so easy to get into!

Did you know, for instance, that the amount of depressed people sulking around the U.S. outnumbers joggers 9-1?

Add to that the catatonics, the out-of-sorts, the crestfallen, those in the doldrums, those in Cincinnati, the disheartened and the generally glum and you're lucky enough to be in some pretty miserable company!

Henrietta Travers of Flint, Michigan writes, "Since following your program, I have become self-pitying, sullen and increasingly anxious in the company of waxed fruit. Thank you. Thank you!"

And you can become an exciting success story too. Just think of it, all those lonely nights at the Horn and Hardhart, talking to your bottle of ketchup!

But first you have to believe in yourself. In your unlimited capacity to become a Truly Depressed Person. You have to wake up each morning, see that sunlight streaming through the window, and go back to sleep.

Now you've got the idea. Instead of building yourself up, knock yourself down. Ask yourself, "What did I do wrong today? How did I screw up?"

Can you do that?

Then congratulations. You've mastered the initial steps. But to earn your prestigious D.D. (Doctorate of Depression) at the end of this handbook, much more hard work is required.

CAUTION: There will be times, of course, when you might suspect that life is worthwhile. That's O.K. Everyone experiences those same kind of fears. They're nothing to be ashamed of.

Through the following chapters a vigorous and specific program will be outlined. You will learn why inertia is the best medicine. How to project negative charisma. How to live in a shell and love it. Withdrawal for fun and profit. And why, astrologically, Leos make the best hostages.

You will be taught how to eat for depression, exercise for depression, meditate for depression, the body language of depression, the exciting history of depression as well as the games depressed people play.

And as if all this weren't depressing enough, you will also learn the secrets of financial insecurity, sexual inadequacy, alcoholic dependency, downward mobility, overcoming the effects of a healthy childhood, and all while working on your losing tennis serve!

We will list where depressed people meet, what they say, what they wear, how they style their hair—and which antidepressants they avoid.

Plus, step-by-step, we will show you how to get a divorce for less than $100.00 (from reality!).

All right. We know you just can't wait to get started. There's a big, wide, wonderful world out there. One which you'll never see. So crawl under the covers. Get into the fetal position. Have an anxiety attack and...

REMEMBER:

Today is the best day of the rest of your life!!

2. DETERMINING YOUR AQ (APATHY QUOTIENT)

Yes, the world is full of grim headlines and disturbing facts. There are burning issues of immense social and political consequence, but that's not the point. The point is are you going to take a stand? Raise your voice and be heard? That's right! Are you finally willing to get up and do something about the deplorable state of affairs which threaten to engulf our whole planet in war, chaos and inconceivable anarchy!?

Well, hopefully not.

For one of the most promising signs that you've become a Truly Depressed Person is the ability to withdraw from reality and become a member of the legume family. (Of course, there are those who withdraw slightly further and become members of the Osmond family.)

However, in the event you do give a damn about anything this exam will quickly ferret it out, because it's a precise and scientific measure of your overall capacity to give up. But where does this special aptitude come from? The answer becomes obvious once we define our terms and their roots:

APATHETIC = A/PATHETIC
(much as THERAPIST = THE/RAPIST)

From this, the next series of ten questions will determine just how much of a/pathetic you really are. It's been carefully devised to measure whether or not you have the ability to successfully obtain employment as a coat tree.

CAUTION: After the exam, some of you may be abject, and some of you may be crestfallen. Others may not be that lucky.

OK. It's that simple. So for each question select the appropriate response. Afterwards, you will be given an opportunity to evaluate your lack of standing. Begin.*

1. A ROSEN IN THE SUN

— Controversial Broadway play about a poor Jewish family that tries to move into a rich black neighborhood.

☐ **TRUE**
☐ **FALSE**
☐ **WHO CARES?**

*NOTE: Those too apathetic to take the test pass automatically and should wait in the closet until further instructions.

18

2. PRE-COLUMBIAN GRASS

— According to former white house aides, a type of marijuana once smoked by Ronald Reagan.

☐ TRUE
☐ FALSE
☐ WHO CARES?

3. FREUDIAN PODIATRY

— A popular new type of therapy in which the analyst gives both emotional, and arch, support.

☐ TRUE
☐ FALSE
☐ WHO CARES?

4. DESIGNER GENES

— What Calvin Klein recently donated to a sperm bank (Semen Savings).

☐ TRUE
☐ FALSE
☐ WHO CARES?

5. MIME KAMPF

— The shocking, recently discovered memoirs of a nonverbal Nazi.

☐ TRUE
☐ FALSE
☐ WHO CARES?

6. "I'VE LOOKED AT LOVE FROM BOTH SIDES NOW"

— Soon-to-be-released single from Christine Jorgensen.

☐ TRUE
☐ FALSE
☐ WHO CARES?

7. LOBOTOMY

— Radical surgical procedure by which the southern hemisphere of the brain is removed (in Australians, the northern hemisphere).

☐ TRUE
☐ FALSE
☐ WHO CARES?

8. JUAN PERIGNON

— Among yuppies, a trendy new champagne imported from Mexico.

☐ TRUE
☐ FALSE
☐ WHO CARES?

9. 1997

— According to a recent FDA report, the year by which they'll be nothing left to eat, except Shelley Winters.

☐ TRUE
☐ FALSE
☐ WHO CARES?

10. THE GOULASH ARCHIPELAGO

— Novel that tells the story of a Russian dissident who, for sixteen years, is forced to eat nothing but Hungarian food.

◻ **TRUE**
◻ **FALSE**
◻ **WHO CARES?**

BONUS QUESTION!

11. PLATO'S RETREAD

—Bronx auto body shop frequented by swingers*

◻ **TRUE**
◻ **FALSE**
◻ **WHO CARES?**

*Particularly after small gender-benders.

ANSWERS

If you answered the questions at all, you fail miserably, and that includes answering "WHO CARES?" as well. However, for each question you didn't answer at all, give yourself 20 points.

Add up your score to determine your AQ. Have you done that? Well, you fail again. Because you should be so a/pathetic that you couldn't care less.

Very well.

If you must, check your AQ below.

NOW CHECK YOUR RATING

AQ	CLASSIFICATION	COMMENTS
160-200	SUB-CATATONIC	Wow! Congratulations! Habitual watcher of "Celebrity Bowling;" fascinated by paper weights; perfect Civil Service material!
120-159	PRE-NEANDERTHAL	Exceptional. Strong advocate of transcendental vegetation; addicted to wise-crack, a drug made from distilled potato chips; interests include sleeping, snoozing and taking naps whenever possible.
80-119	V.D. (Very Dormant)	Just average. Fond of rolling eyes at mutual-fund salesmen; thinks casual sex means having to wear a leisure suit during intercourse; constantly dreams of Hoboken.

AQ	CLASSIFICATION	COMMENTS
40-79	FANATICAL AMBIVALENT	Pretty poor. Classical macho type—needs a machete to remove nose hair; responds to people of wit and intelligence by imitating a wurst; has a lusty appetite for immersing typing school graduates in sour cream.
0-39	P.O. (PATHOLOGICAL OPTIMIST)	Utter failure! Probably has a Ph.D. from Columbia or an IUD from Yale; likes to jog around wet laundry till it dries; prefers wearing grey slacks when being introduced to sheep. By the way, if married, has a wife that's absolutely first rate, although her rates go up after 8:00 P.M.

3. YOUR HORROR SCOPE

Why is there no hope, or chance of salvation, or a clean restroom along the New York State Thruway? Why do some men have cats for pets, and others Christie Brinkley?

Well, as most of us who are adult and irrational have already come to accept, the stars have a great influence on our day-to-day misfortunes. That's why Truly Depressed People leave no stone unturned in trying to understand the complex planetary factors responsible for such horrid events as plague, pestilence, and root-canal work. Moreover, they know we are insignificant blobs of protoplasm doomed to wander through a cruel and indifferent universe, though things are slightly worse in Newark.

For this reason, those who are Truly Depressed People will consult their astrological charts before taking a trip, making a commitment, or buying a pants suit made of Naugahyde.

So be forewarned.

The following will shed new light on the Cosmic factors that are responsible for our dark moods and lousy luck. Like other charts, it will be divided into twelve signs, (thirteen, if you were born under a Stop sign.) But unlike other charts, it will offer no assurance or solace whatsoever.

Now look up your birthday to see what dismal prognostications your zodiac configuration foretells!

CAPRICORN

December 22 - January 20

You're in touch with reality, but it's a long distance call. You're careless and impractical and don't take risks, like changing the sheets on your bed. All your internal organs are on the outside. Your wife will run off with a shoehorn repairman. Someone close will try to poison you. Avoid croissants.

KEY NUMBERS

-6, 213, 457, 936.02, and pi

IMPERSONAL NOTE

Not capable of owning your own feelings, you lease them instead.

WHOM YOU ATTRACT

Individuals born under the sign of Neon.

AQUARIUS

January 21 - February 19

Thinking yourself pure, you sleep on a waterbed filled with Perrier. People are always finding new depths to your superficiality. Failing to keep up the payments to your local exorcist, you will be repossessed. The White Knights of B'Nai B'rith will burn a six foot matzoh on your lawn. Aquarians make the best bus drivers.

INSIGNIFICANT DAYS

January 1st to December 31st.

SPECIAL NOTE

If you were born on the 17th or 23rd between four and six A.M., eight to ten P.M. or noon and two P.M., your '62 Buick will be stolen.

ANSWER TO A PROBABLE QUESTION

Yes, you are gay.

PISCES

February 20th - March 20th

Pluto indicates that your life is an exercise in futility but that's OK, you need the exercise. From the 5th to the 13th, reluctance to talk about personal problems will only make those around you ecstatic. Co-workers remark that if you had any more substance, you'd be two-dimensional. Visit someone who is under the earth.

FLASH!

You will be instrumental in helping a Soviet scientist defect to Russia!

MEDICAL NOTE

On the 18th you will become the first human being to be successfully cloned, although this will leave you beside yourself.

WHOM YOU ATTRACT

Individuals born under the sign of Caesarean.

ARIES

March 21st - April 20th

Politically, you're confused, and favor returning the Suez Canal to Panama. On the 11th there'll be a dinner at a German/Chinese restaurant but, an hour later, you'll get hungry for power. Problems encountered this week can be solved with concern, communication, and a crowbar. The 21st and 22nd are truly expansive days and you will be imbued with a new feeling of energy — after your toaster electrocutes you.

HEAVY VIBES

Your girlfriend will gain so much weight that she'll break your heart, as well as numerous park benches.

ACHTUNG!

Around the 19th, a German commandant may try to moor a zeppelin to your nose.

ON THE NEGATIVE SIDE

When Venus enters your seventh house you will be sued for palimony by a woman you used to live with — in a previous lifetime.

TAURUS

April 21st - May 21st

Socially, you're very cautious, which explains why you even put a condom over the receiver during phone sex. This is the time of year for doing something really special for a loved one. Like leaving. A surprise invitation will come your way around the 14th, from the D.A. The eclipse of the moon on the 23rd indicates that it's very important for you to remain grounded to your work—as a lightning rod. Be ready for a collect call. From Tito.

KEY NUMBERS

911, 555-1212, "0"

CONGRATULATIONS!

On May 9th you'll be awarded the Nobel Prize for Literature. Posthumously.

ANSWER TO A PROBABLE QUESTION

Maybe. Maybe not. Well, maybe.

GEMINI

May 22nd - June 21st

A bright spark ignites the first week of this month. Your son is a pyromaniac. Midweek will bring a subtle change in the atmosphere when your sweat socks begin to mildew. A top modeling agency will claim that your face has definition but no meaning. On the 17th and 18th, the moon is in your sign of the zodiac suggesting a new career—as a toll collector on the Ho Chi Minh trail.

HEALTH NOTE

The week of the 23rd your soft palate will turn hard.

HIGHLIGHT

During the 6th and 7th your personal magnetism will be very strong, pulling the fillings out of people's teeth.

CONFIDENTIAL

As a woman you have everything a man would want, though not in the places he'd expect to find them.

CANCER

June 22nd - July 23rd

As the week of the 23rd draws nearer you'll begin to form new social contacts, at a VD clinic. Now is the time to turn creative energy into stress. Others find that you have a definite Neptunian aura, probably from not using a deodorant. Last week of the month should be utilized for settling a rift at home, planning repairs, and removing your frontal lobes.

ROMANTIC NOTE

Mercury indicates that your fiancee believes in premarital divorce.

MUSICAL NOTE

E-flat.

FLASH!

Around the latter part of the month a UFO will save your marriage, when it kidnaps your Mother-in-Law.

LEO

July 24th - August 23rd

During the interval of the 14th through the 23rd, you will be consumed with feelings of self-loathing, despair and despondency; however, on the 24th, things will begin to get worse. The moon is in your sign of the zodiac suggesting that a Capricorn will be entering your wife. All planets point to the fact that the University of Notre Dame will soon offer you a scholarship (to play hunchback). Leos make the best hostages.

PLANETARY NOTE

A solar eclipse occurs at 3:56 P.M. on the 23rd, so be ready to take a shower.

FLASH!

Around the 30th or 31st an old friend will run into you — with a snowplow.

WHOM YOU ATTRACT

Bail bondsmen.

UNSUCCESSFUL SUICIDE ATTEMPT WITH ELECTRIC RAZOR

VIRGO

August 24th - September 23rd

Painful memories will surface around the 17th and you will recall the time that you were too short to make the debating team. A noted plastic surgeon will disclosure that the only way you could get a face lift is with a derrick. Pluto indicates that a suicide attempt will end unsuccessfully, after three weeks of trying to slash your wrists with an electric razor.

CONFIDENTIAL

Meditate on a situation that's been bothering you (but get up before he suffocates).

CAUTION

This month history repeats itself, especially if you've been to a Mexican restaurant the night before.

ROMANTIC NOTE

From the 13th to the 27th, animal magnetism surges to the point where even dead cats follow you home.

LIBRA

September 24th - October 23rd

Friends refuse to let you denigrate yourself, because they insist on doing it themselves. With your drive and ability there's no doubt that you'll rise from the working class, and eventually become a manual laborer. The 25th and 26th should be earmarked for more pleasurable pursuits, such as spreading anchovies over a lumberjack. Rejoice! Someone you have always loved will finally be warming up to you—at your cremation. Libras make the best excuses.

LEGAL NOTE

If you were born between 2:00 and 6:00 A.M. then you will be convicted of trying to sell arms to Iran, as well as a few legs.

PERSONAL NOTE

On the night of the 30th, during the full moon, a Times Square psychic will massage your astral body.

RELATIVE MATTERS

To help celebrate your mother's birthday, you'll sing to her legs, "You're So Vein."

SCORPIO

October 24th - November 22nd

Starting on the 29th, your moon will enter Sagittarius, from the rear. Lovers are especially impressed by the ability to lick your eyebrows with your tongue. During a bio-lab party, a new outfit will evoke giggles from fetal piglets. Between the 25th and 27th, there is a strong chance that Immigration may declare you an illegal alien and that you will be deported — to Alpha Centauri.

RED ALERT!

If you are black, and living in the Soviet Union, you will come down with Hammer and Sickle Cell Anemia.

VERY PERSONAL NOTE

You're so insecure that, even when you masturbate, you fake orgasm.

CAUTION

The Forces of Darkness are closing in, so pay your electric bill.

SAGITTARIUS

November 23rd - December 21st

The sign of Mercury in your seventh house indicates that in the 60's you were known to drop a lot of acid—especially on the carpet. November 11th, a crazed veterinarian will attempt to neuter your poodle with a croquet mallet. At a sperm bank, a teller will offer to lend you a hand. And, after the 23rd there'll be a marked change in your attitude towards the environment. You'll be in solitary.

INTELLECTUAL NOTE

If ignorance is bliss, then you should be in ecstasy.

PSYCHOLOGICAL NOTE

You're psycho-ceramic. A crackpot.

WHOM YOU ATTRACT

A Leo with Penis rising.

4. GREAT MOMENTS IN DEPRESSION

> "He who does not remember the past
> is condemned to forgetting where he parked."
> —*anonymous used car dealer.*

The history of man is written in blood, which may explain why so many of our ancestors were anemic. There has been misery and woe of every possible description, greed and cruelty beyond belief, with occasional time off to watch Monday night football.

Since the dawn of time, and maybe even a little earlier for those with insomnia, archaeologists, paleontologists and urologists have all searched for the answers. What are the common threads that tie Stone Age Man, Bronze Age Man and Middle-Aged Man together, and how can you get these threads wholesale?

Yes, even the ancient troglodytes celebrated Time Immemorial Day and got a three day weekend set aside for rest, relaxation and barbecuing neighboring tribes. So read it and weep! Recall the plight of the Pre-Raphaelites* who never even realized they came before Raphael. And feel for the anguish of Samuel Furfooz, a historian who spent nearly thirty years searching for the missing link, between Route 17 and Interstate 80.

No, it's not hard. The events of the past provide constant inspiration for those who seek to be depressed in the future. For instance:

317,469 B.C. (Before Circumcision)

Townsend Groc, noted cliff dweller, distraught over his failure to market a passable brontosaurus pâté, refuses to leave his cave. His wife Bernice, disgruntled, runs off with a petrified florist.

5467 B.C.

Muffy Nefertiti, the first Egyptian princess to be named Muffy, sneaks out of the palace and goes down to a local tavern where she drinks, in quick succession, a Cheops on the Rocks, a Moses Mimosa and a Red Sea Spritzer.

While inebriated, she begins to scribble some of her most intimate thoughts on a papyrus napkin, which eventually becomes the best selling novel "Mummy Dearest."

---

*Author's note: That's Juan Raphael, a Mexican housepainter who lived circa 1926, and who also wrote the immensely popular song, "Tiajuana Dance and Hold My Hand."

312 B.C.

Hercules Lanzano, a fearless gladiator, in order to retrieve a joy buzzer that Caesar has dropped, leaps into a pit of ferocious lions and is terribly mauled. The Emperor, recognizing his valor, immediately grants him two weeks severance pay — but the gladiator is unable to sign the check and it's later voided after 90 days.

118 A.D.

Octavious Frivolous (author of "I, Frivolous"), in a fit of rage after overhearing a remark that asserted he had a "Christian" nose, revokes tax deductions for all those who ever claimed a three-martini orgy.

1287 A.D.

Aria Rugg, a receptionist for the Ottoman Empire, upset at having to work overtime during the Hundred Years' War, disconnects all Baghdad, causing chaos, revolution, and a small decline in halvah production.

1582 A.D.

Laconic the Elder, ruler of Corsica and student of American foreign policy in the thirteenth century, enacts a decree that forever bans alternate side of the street famines. His subjects rejoice, and no one is ever again towed away between 8:00 A.M. and 6:00 P.M. for starving illegally.

1944 A.D.

Flaming Teriyaki, the infamous drag queen turned kamikaze pilot, misses a U.S. aircraft carrier and plunges into the Tokyo home of Ghengis Cohen (the martial-arts film star noted for his ability to cripple his adversaries with lightning guilt).* Neither man survives but, miraculously, police do manage to rescue the film star's five year old Sony.

---

*Ghengis is also a close friend of Bruce Lee (short for Lebowitz).

1979 A.D.

Alfie Centauri, and other emissaries of a super-advanced alien race, attempt to deliver a message before the United Nations that details how to end war, disease, and the small portions served in French restaurants, but they cannot find a parking space and instead are forced to take in the local scenery, until their vehicle is full and they return.

1988 A.D.

Lester Ferko, a marketing consultant specializing in Bolivian water, undergoes the world's first pubic hair transplant. Although the operation is widely considered a success, it's observed that whenever a beautiful woman passes, his head has a tendency to come to a point.

5. The Low Sugar/High Valium Diet

Some depressed women believe that the best way to a man's heart is through his stomach, though most prefer going directly through his rib cage. Yes, it's a fact that everybody knows. Good food is like good sex, except you rarely have to put a condom over a bread stick unless, of course, you're dining in certain restaurants on the upper west side of Chad.

Today, many of our present attitudes about food and depression date back to the time of the French Revolution when Marie Antoinette, in the midst of dieting, uttered the now famous words, "Let them eat rice cakes." Several years later she became a popular singer and instantly rocketed to success with the tune "Raindrops Keep Falling On My Head," but that's neither here nor there.

Today, depressed people are a nervous, anxious lot, abandoned by the government, organized religion, as well as their dry cleaners, who promised them their shirts by Thursday. Unable to experience pleasure, even after sixteen helpings of pie a la mode, they demand culinary fare that at least has a tranquilizing effect.

ERICA SCHLONG'S "FEAR OF FRYING"

Luckily, their cries have been heard by Erica Schlong, whose cookbook, "Fear of Frying," has become an instant hit. (Erica's two previous successes were "The Maintenance Diet," a program in which dieters were required to report to a local filling station every 5,000 tacos to get their mouths realigned, and "The Rigid Diet Plan," which advised thousands of people all over the country to rest, stay in bed and drink plenty of embalming fluids.)

According to Ms. Schlong, there has only been one reported incidence of anyone ever recovering from her diets and that occurred in Fargo, North Dakota, where a tailor was secretly found in a compromising position with a boiled chicken.

On most diets, the depressed take out their hostility on defenseless cucumbers, often going downstairs in the middle of the night and circumcising them. However, on the "Low Sugar/High Valium" diet, they are incapable of this type of behavior because only the purest ingredients are used, such as eggs, flour, and the finest Novocaine sugar. That's right. Each recipe is guaranteed to be completely unhealthful and unappetizing.

Additionally, for those depressed folks who are concerned that they are not getting enough chloresterol or saturated fat in their diet, Ms. Schlong has included some delicacies that reflect the popular shift towards inorganic cooking, such as "Quaalude Quiche."

Yet whatever your lack of taste, this epicurean menu is sure to debilitate even the most hearty gastronome. Following are six classic favorites, contributed by Ms. Schlong, who not only finds time to serve great food, but 25 years to life as well.

6. YOGA FOR DEPRESSION

Simultaneously, more than four thousand years ago, the people of Nepal, India, and Jersey City developed a series of postures and breathing exercises to promote deep and profound levels of nausea.

They believed that in the air itself there existed an energy source called Pruna, from which all yeast infections sprang. Realizing that we probably do not get enough of this Pruna in our daily lives, they created a system of chest and abdominal movements designed to expand our capacity to diminish the quality of our lives.

The following series of exercises constitutes a daily regimen that should be performed twenty minutes after our morning meal, twenty minutes after our evening meal, and twenty minutes after our last meal.

"If you are already clear, these exercises will make you perfectly transparent."

—*Swami Baba Ganoush*

EXERCISE #1: ANXIETY TWIST

OBJECTIVE:

A gentle way to relax the back and neck by slowly severing the spinal chord.

PRACTICE INFORMATION

Fig. 1. First sit with your legs outstretched and cross your left leg over your right as illustrated. Place your left hand on the floor firmly behind your back. Cross your right arm over your left knee and take hold of your right knee.

Fig. 2. Very slowly, without moving your trunk, twist your head 360 degrees. Don't stop. Twist it all the way around again. Hold this position for a count of ten days. Now do the same thing in the opposite direction.

Fig. 3. Following the final repetition, turn forward, stretch your legs, relax, and let your head fall off.

As you can see, the precepts and practice of yoga date back to dim antiquity, a much simpler and holistic time when not only great philosophies were born, but so was Ronald Reagan.

The ancient gurus proclaimed that the main objective of life should be physical, mental, and spiritual harmony, with some time off to improve one's credit rating.

Yet above all, for discovering true peace of mind, the science of yoga offers a direct path to the inner self, provided it doesn't cut across your neighbor's lawn.

The following exercise will demonstrate this.

FIG. 1

FIG. 2

FIG. 3

EXERCISE #2: BACKWARD BREAK

OBJECTIVE:

To promote good circulation and stimulation of the thyroid gland through a series of controlled movements and slipped discs.

Practice Information:

Fig. 1. Lie face down with your chin resting comfortably on the mat. Remember, it is essential to perform each motion gracefully.

Fig. 2. Simultaneously, lift the back legs together with your head and shoulders. Bring them both to a 90 degree angle to the floor. Experience the stretching in your rib cage and thighs.

Fig. 3. Continue the lifting process, arching your head and legs, until the backs of your heels and the front of your nose have exchanged places.

NOTE: This exercise not only benefits your endocrine system, but your chiropractor as well.

The entire routine of the next three exercises can be done in five years or less, if you get time off for good behavior. Many devotees perform these exercises after rising, taking a shower, or committing adultery.

Indeed yoga, above all other beliefs, stresses the need for complete and total harmony, especially among certain rock groups.

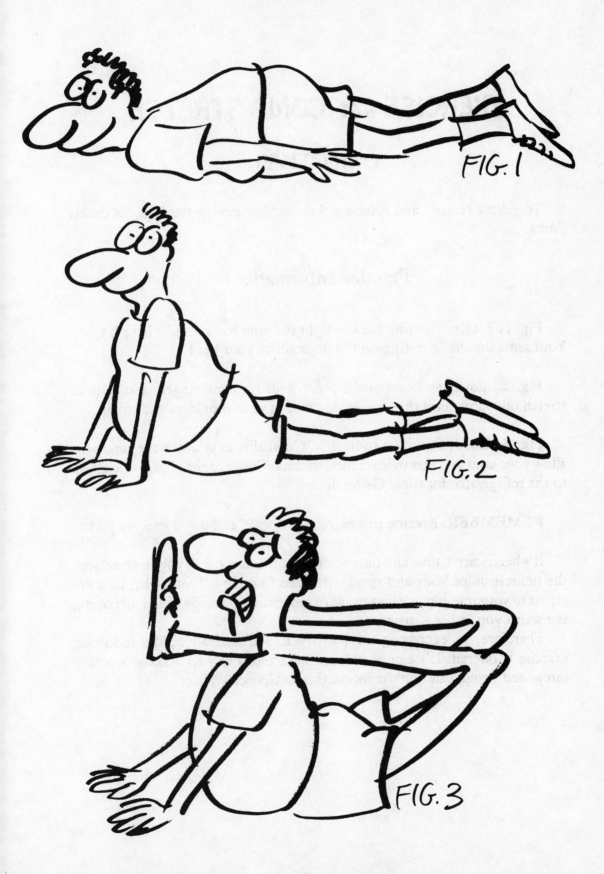

FIG. 1

FIG. 2

FIG. 3

EXERCISE #3: COMA STRETCH

OBJECTIVE:

To relieve tension and promote flexibility by freeing the body of excess limbs.

Practice Information:

Fig. 1. Lie flat with your back straight and your feet shoulder length apart. Your arms should be resting on the floor above your head.

Fig. 2. Slowly and cautiously, point your toes and fingers and start to stretch outwards. Feel the tension decrease in your shoulders and thighs.

Fig. 3. Good. Continue to stretch. Gradually, as you breathe regularly, allow your arms and legs to leave their sockets. Count to ten. Then wriggle up to the refrigerator for some Gatorade.

REMEMBER: Execute this exercise properly, and it will execute you.

It's been stated, time and time again, that the purpose of yoga is to achieve the unification of body and mind with East Germany. That's why, in every aspect of your training, it's important to move with grace, provided, of course, she wants you in her apartment.

Therefore, to expedite your journey to self-realization, the following exercise is offered. It's a powerful and miraculous way to become a totally integrated being, but don't mention this to George Wallace.

FIG. 1

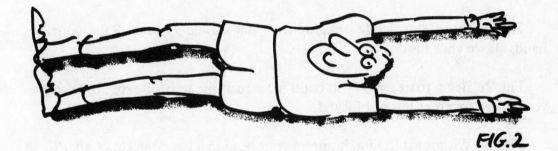

FIG. 2

FIG. 3

EXERCISE #4: INCOMPLETE BREATH

OBJECTIVE:

To make each intake of air long and shallow, gradually decreasing the frequency of breathing till respiration stops entirely.

Practice Information:

Fig. 1. Stand completely straight with your shoulders back. Raise your hands above your head.

Fig. 2. Begin to exhale as you bend forward at the waist. Be sure to keep your knees together but not locked.

Fig. 3. Without stopping, immerse your head in a large bucket of goat's milk and inhale. Completely fill your lungs with the liquid in a slow, rhythmic manner. Count to 35,000.

NOTE: This exercise need only be performed once.

In the following exercise, special attention is paid to the kidneys, bladder and colon, or, if you're a writer, the semicolon. It provides a tranquilizing effect that many students have equated with spiritual peace, nirvana, or two sixpacks and a bottle of Valium.

Remember to always practice it 5 times in a seated position, 10 times in a standing position, and 20 times in a compromising position.

FIG.1   FIG.2   FIG.3

EXERCISE #5: MOOSHU'S POSTURE

OBJECTIVE:

To provide an intensive rupture of the spleen. Performed inside a thin pancake.

Practice Information:

Fig. 1. Stand up straight with both feet on the floor. Practice tensing your abdominal muscles to get some control over them.

Fig. 2. Start to exhale. Contract the abdominal muscles by pulling in your stomach. Feel the lower rib cage raise as the pelvis area becomes taut.

Fig. 3. Don't stop. Use the diaphragm muscles in your chest, as well as the muscles of the lower back, to aid in the contraction. Continue until your waist measures 3/8".

NOTE: The problem of constipation has almost been entirely eliminated by using this exercise.

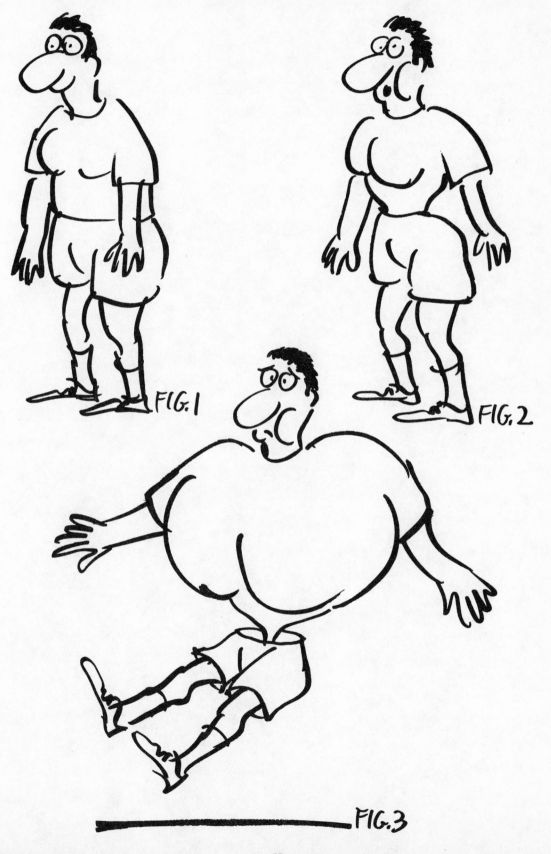

FIG. 1

FIG. 2

FIG. 3

7. THE SENSUOUS CATATONIC

(A Gourmet Guide to Complete Withdrawal)

> **"An orgasm in the hand
> is worth two in the bush."**
>
> —*Dr. Phyllis Phallus, Director,*
> *New School for Social Disease*

Do you have trouble maintaining flaccidity? Does your lover know how to bring you to anticlimax? If asked, could you give your partner a tender and loving spinal tap? Can you define the term "Anal-Repulsive"?*

If any of these questions touch a delicate area, don't be alarmed, for becoming a Sensuous Catatonic requires years and years of Insensitivity Training. What turns one person off may turn another on and that could be a disaster. Here then, are some general pointers you should follow.

First, partners should take long, tender moments exploring every aspect of each other's bodies, until they eventually lose interest. After that, it's important to communicate all the fantasies you've never told another living soul, including the one about being spanked by a Postal employee.

Finally, though most women don't like to admit it, the man should take the initiative, and leave.

As you can see, there's no reason why even the healthiest couples can't have a wonderfully inactive sex life. The following rules are designed to help facilitate a lack of mutual respect and increase nonorgasmic levels:

CREDO OF THE SENSUOUS CATATONIC

1. The Sensous Catatonic knows there is nothing more beautiful than finding out their partner's needs, and ignoring them.

2. The Sensuous Catatonic understands that a woman's greatest asset, after her natural perfume, is her trust fund.

3. The Sensuous Catatonic knows how to inspire genuine feedback from their partner using only patience, love, and a cattle prod.

4. The Sensuous Catatonic has such low self-esteem that, even when he masturbates, he has performance anxiety.

*obnoxious proctologist

5. The Sensuous Catatonic realizes that smell probably has more to do with sexual repulsion than anything else.

Above all, the important thing is to be imaginative. Playful. Women, during foreplay, often fail to use enough pressure with their handwork. This can be corrected by using a vise. On the other hand, male strength should be asserted, not only with brute strength or bear hugs, but with caring, concern and occasionally some ether. Skin, hair, armpits, breasts, these are all Irrelevant Zones and should be avoided, though you are allowed to touch each other's toothbrush.

IRRELEVANT ZONES

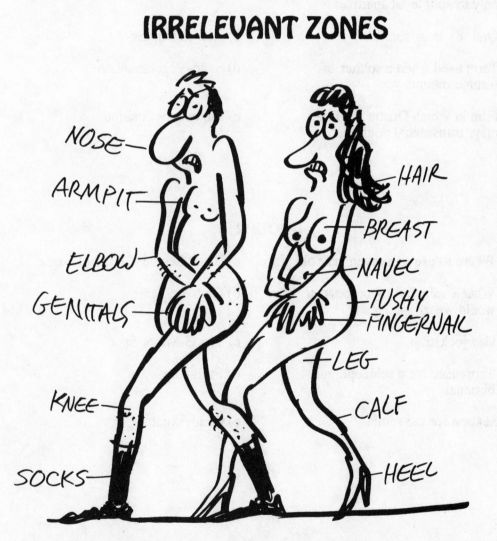

O.K. You've got the basics. You know that if it feels good, deny it. But to see how much of a gourmet you really are, the following test has been devised. It covers a wide range of topics that every Sensuous Catatonic should know about.

MATCH THE DEFINITIONS IN COLUMN "A" WITH THEIR TERMS IN COLUMN "B".

GROUP 1

1. Flagellation with a hot zucchini

a) Footsie

2. A venereal disease transmitted only in split level apartments

b) Con Job

3. Oral sex in prison.

c) Herpes Duplex

4. Term used when a soldier-of-fortune mounts you

d) Sado-Vegetarianism

5. Film in which Dustin Hoffman plays transsexual podiatrist

e) Mercenary Position

GROUP 2

1. Where to excite a seven year old girl

a) Black Leather Contact Lenses

2. What a vain, but myopic sadist would wear

b) Club Medicare

3. Gay jockstrap

c) The G-Minor Spot

4. Term used for a schizophrenic bisexual

d) Fruit Cup

5. Sex spa for the senile

e) Quadsexual

GROUP 3

1. Uncircumcised rock group	a) Well-Rung
2. Lamb into S&M	b) "Safe" Sex
3. What his female lovers claim Quasimodo to be	c) Half and Half's
4. Milk bar for hermaphrodites	d) Mutton for Punishment
5. Intercourse within a locked vault	e) The Four Skins

GROUP 4

FROM THE STORY OUTLINE GIVEN IN COLUMN "A," IDENTIFY THE PORNO FILM IN COLUMN "B."

A	B
1. The satanic sex habits of a former President's mother	a) Behind the Revolving Door
2. A transsexual can't make up his/her mind	b) Debbie Does Logarithms
3. Mathematical nympho performs naked functions	c) Brief Encounter With Kinds
4. Aliens land at Plato's Retreat	d) Deep Bagel
5. Intimate portrayal of the illicit affair between a rabbi and his breakfast	e) The Devil in Miss Lillian

(ANSWERS ON NEXT PAGE)

ANSWERS

GROUP 1	GROUP 2	GROUP 3	GROUP 4
1. d	1. c	1. e	1. e
2. c	2. a	2. d	2. a
3. b	3. d	3. a	3. b
4. e	4. e	4. c	4. c
5. a	5. b	5. b	5. d

Now add up the number of right answers and check below.

#RIGHT	CATEGORY	FAVORITE SEXUAL ACT
16-20	AUTO-EROTIC	Menage a trois with a Volkswagen.
12-15	SADO-PERIODONTAL	Being bound and severely flossed by a dental hygienist.
8-11	PEKING TOM	Doing it "Chinese Style" with a sweet and sour dwarf.
4-7	NECRO-AMPHIBIAN	Giving frogs whirlpools in Waring blenders.
0-3	NASAL-COMPULSIVE	Likes to climax by having nose blown.

8. WHAT COLOR IS YOUR PARANOIA?

All over the country, people are extremely panicky that their phone has been tapped by the Dutch Secret Service. Many others are concerned that their condos—in Miami Beach—have been targeted as ground zero.

Even more frightening, there's a growing number of individuals haunted by the knowledge that the same person who killed JFK, Marilyn Monroe and Dr. Martin Luther King, also taught them the accordion.

Well, from both a psychological and an analytical point-of-view, these are perfectly reasonable fears.

However, in order to become a Truly Depressed Person, you're going to have to acquire a whole new set of anxieties. But before we go any further, let's answer some commonly asked questions about paranoia:

CAN HAVING ENEMIES CAUSE PARANOIA?

This is a controversial issue to which we don't yet have all the answers. Recent studies have indicated that hypersensitivity to persecution will lead to paranoia in some people. However, it's more likely that most paranoia probably stems from allergic reactions to carpet sweepings or gypsies.

IS PARANOIA THE RESULT OF A CHEMICAL IMBALANCE?

All thoughts and feelings, including those centering on Swedish twins and a can of Cheese Whip, are caused by chemicals within the brain. These complex electrochemical reactions occur over and over in every one of the three billion people on this planet, except for jockeys.

Some doctors believe paranoia is a result of adrenal and pituitary disturbances, however, others believe it's a disturbance caused by Armenians picketing your home.

Whatever the case, it's foolish and unwise to wait for a chemical imbalance to impart the feeling that you're constantly being mocked by woodchucks.

HOW COMMON IS PARANOIA?

Of the more than 200 million Americans alive today, over half, at sometime in their life, will be convinced that leprechauns are attempting to steal their pinwheel hats. For just as hair color, eye color, and the color of one's ties are genetically determined, so is paranoia.

In fact, researchers have recently isolated the chromosome responsible for persecution complexes in men who insist on wearing lobster bibs to hockey games.

Also, some intriguing test results have been reported about those who feel they are being secretly mooned by Teamsters but, at the moment, these are inconclusive.

WHAT ARE THE SYMPTOMS OF HYPERPARANOIA?

Hyper (too much) paranoia (two noia's) is a state of heightened fear and anxiety, frequently triggered by aluminum siding salesmen. In this state hyperventilation occurs, which is marked by rapid breathing, a fast pulse, and small air vents popping up along the face and neck.

Many times, hyperparanoids can also be identified by their constant shivering and shaking, which accounts for their popularity as lead singers in rumba bands.

In Hawaiians, particularly, this same anxious state can be induced by the Don making you an offer you can't refuse though, quite frequently, this merely turns out to Don Ho.

WILL PARANOIA DAMAGE MY HEALTH?

Unfortunately, there's no justification for this kind of optimism. Paranoids frequently go for years without developing high blood pressure, ulcers, asthma, and they often have to settle for a complexion not unlike eggplant salad.

In a recent development, a study of hospital charts at the University of Idaho Medical Center found that 72% of all paranoid men and women, involved in fatal accidents, died.

CAN TRAUMATIC EXPERIENCES CAUSE PARANOIA?

Most definitely. In the following case studies, we'll see just how paranoid personalities are formed:

CASE STUDY #1

NAME: Harold Kaputnik

AGE: 31

OCCUPATION: Manufacturer of nylons for frog's legs

"I have a fear of speaking in front of large groups of herrings. Often, this includes just stating my name, my age, or even my hat size. As far back as I can remember, I've had similar problems.

My mother used to force me to treat cans of tuna fish with courtesy and once even spanked me when I failed to tip my hat to an order of smelts.

In high school, the first event that caused me great stress was in hygiene class, where I was forced to resuscitate a guppy. Later, as a college undergraduate, I had no problems until my junior year, when I suddenly realized that I was attending a school for minnows."

CASE STUDY #2

NAME: Mike Muscatel

AGE: 45

OCCUPATION: Teaches anatomy of fowl to chicken pluckers

"I have a morbid fear of contracting cancer, which is only exceeded by a morbid fear of contracting carpenters. Recently, though, this fear has extended to electricians and now I will even cross the street when I see a plumber walking in my direction. In fact, I won't even visit people who have plumbing in their homes. Luckily, most of my friends don't."

CASE STUDY #3

NAME: Diane Airbus
AGE: 57
OCCUPATION: Delivering babies (though now she's experiencing a
             midwife crisis)

"When I was three or four years old, I suddenly became afraid of Peter, Paul and Mary. I don't recall any specific incident that led to it, except that my mother had been bitten by a folk singer. Generally, it's not much of a problem because I tend to avoid places, like coffeehouses and parks, where people are known to associate with guitars.

Yesterday, however, was the worst day of my life. I went to the bathroom and there I saw John Denver taking a shower. I was paralyzed with fear and incapable of leaving the room until my husband came home and dried him off."

Of course, some of you may not have the natural advantages of traumatic experiences, glandular imbalances or being born Richard Nixon to help induce paranoia. If this is the case, you should study the following list to find a paranoid disorder you can call your own.

1. SUSHI-NOIA: A crippling fear, borrowed from the Japanese, that raw fish are whispering behind your back.

2. GRECO-PHRENIA: The uneasy suspicion that you are being persecuted by Greek waiters (usually occurs after requesting a second cup of coffee).

☆   ☆   ☆

3. POST-FATAL DEPRESSION: A morbid dread affecting the recently deceased; the rude awakening that there really is a hell.

☆   ☆   ☆

4. FEAR OF KOOL-AIDS: Preoccupation with catching a deadly disease from a gay eskimo.

☆   ☆   ☆

5. NERVELESS BREAKDOWN: Profound terror of waking up and discovering that, while you slept, all your teeth had root canal work.

☆   ☆   ☆

6. SKIRTZ-O-PHOBIA: A foreboding that besets overweight women; a feeling that construction workers are discussing the pros and cons of your mini.

☆   ☆   ☆

7. MANNEQUIN DEPRESSION: A persistent and numbing fear that most, if not all, of your colleagues consider you a dummy.

☆   ☆   ☆

8. INFANT-O-PHOBIA: Disquiet experienced by middle-aged men; anxiety that their mothers will volunteer to come over and do the laundry.

☆   ☆   ☆

9. DENTAL DISORDER: Severe apprehension suffered by periodontists; fear that it's their conversation, and not the Novocaine, which has a numbing effect.

☆   ☆   ☆

10. MELLOW PANIC: An extreme trepidation known to afflict New Yorkers and others in touch with reality; an unholy dread of having to spend more than two weeks in California.

A SUCCESS STORY

Cynthia de Mentia, a professional flagpole waxer, has been able to acquire all of the above syndromes and she reports the following remarkable results:

"Almost every night, I have a recurring dream where I find myself in a future society ruled by Nazi war criminals and post office workers. In this nightmare world, it is compulsory for every woman, when she turns sixteen, to alter her physical appearance to conform to one of the established norms. Failure to do so means instant death, or banishment to Indianapolis, whichever comes first.

In this dream, I am a plain girl with a wonderful personality who attempts to defy the fate that awaits her within the chamber of transformation. Seeking support, I call upon my mother, sister and school counselor, but they all look like Truman Capote and I get even more confused.

Since there are only thirteen women models to choose from, each with a limited 90 day warranty, I decided to buck the system and fight for the right to have acne until I'm sixty-five. But inexorably the pressure mounts and mounts until my will finally snaps when I'm told that, unless I undergo the metamorphosis, my subscription to Cosmo will be cancelled.

At this point, the dream takes a strange turn. Two clones of Gerald Ford take me to a cold, gray chamber where I'm forced to remove my clothes and sing the Ukrainian national anthem to a ventriloquist. Then, all of a sudden, a switch is thrown and there's blackness, nothing but horrible, absolute, engulfing blackness.

So they change the fuse and start again. In a few seconds I emerge with my body completely transformed, identical to 700 million other women on the planet, except that I still find myself attracted to midget wrestlers. It's here that I usually wake up, only to discover that my bed has been short-sheeted by Danish seamen."

9. EUROPE ON FIVE LIBRIUM A DAY

Are you a romantic? Carefree and young at heart? Do you consider yourself an impassioned wayfarer with an insatiable thirst for new and exotic locales? Hey, you've got a problem!

But one that can be overcome.

For AA (Agoraphobics Anonymous), in conjunction with the NAACP (National Association for the Advancement of Claustro Phobia), has put together a series of tour packages specifically designed to keep you in your room — under the linoleum.

All our clients fly the latest AC/DC-10's (also known as biplanes) and are immediately enrolled in our Frequent Hostage Program, where they quickly accumulate bonus miles good for free one-way tickets to Beirut.

Additionally, for those who may suffer from fear of flying, ocean passage is effortlessly arranged on the vessel recognized as the flagship of depression, the S.S. Doldrums.

However, no matter what mode of transport you choose, we guarantee that our tour packages are designed to let you see this world today — and the next world tomorrow.

NOTE: Prices subject to change without notice. Gratuities, meals, and straitjackets, not included.

1. SEWERS OF PARIS CRUISE

(Seven nights, No days)

The Louvre, Notre Dame, and the Arc de Triomphe are but a few of the city's famous landmarks that we will be passing under during 172 hours of total darkness!

DAY #1
BELOW THE LOUVRE.

DAY #4
SUBMERGED UNDER
NOTRE DAME.

DAY #7
BENEATH THE ARC
D'TRIOMPHE.

10. SINGLES' TOUR OF SIBERIA
(43 Days, 42 Nights)

1st Day: Leave Milwaukee at 5:23 A.M. in a pickup truck. Everyone is bound and gagged. Drive overland to undisclosed location on the Newfoundland coast where an unmarked submarine picks you up.

2nd Day: Under Atlantic

3rd Day: Under North Sea

4th Day: Under Volga River

5th Day: Arrive Kiev 7:34 P.M. Put on blindfolds. On to Burger Czar for dinner.

6th Day: After breakfast, complete tour of Ukraine 9:30-9:35 A.M. Free time to leisurely roam confines of Siberian labor camp, or take romantic stroll through electroshock reorientation center.

7th Day: Tour the countryside in the luxurious comfort of a rebuilt Czech army tank. Some continue by jeep to Afghanistan (optional).

8th Day: See the peasant-under-glass, a special stop at Lenin's Tomb.

9th Day: Board your waiting submarine back to USA. Three quick stops (2 for fuel, 1 to launch surprise missile attack).

10th Day: Under Indian Ocean

11th Day: Under Pacific Ocean

12th Day: Under Kennebunkport, Maine

13th Day: Under Gulf of Mexico

14th Day: Arrive Cuba. Everybody disembarks and boards an overcrowded shrimp boat for connection Miami Beach.

42nd Day: Survivors hitch a ride in Valiant back to Milwaukee.

43rd Day: Arrive Milwaukee 2. Remove blindfolds.

11. RESTAURANT TOUR OF TIAJUANA:

(365 Days, 365 Nights)

A gastronomic holiday! 1 day in Mexico. 364 days in San Diego General for intensive care!!

10.
The National Enema
"America's Most Depressing Paper" (Vol. 1)

10 Top Psychics Predict:
IDI AMIN DESTINED TO REMAIN BLACK!

**"Angel of Death"
Beckoned Me To Buffalo,
Says Man Who Came
Back from Beyond**
★ ★ ★
**REVEALED!
The Secret Feud between
the PLO and Israel**
★ ★ ★
**Most People Don't
Want Crabs**

**Incredible Report Shows
97% Die within Year after Birthday**
★ ★ ★
**How The Color of Your Wife
Reveals Your Personality**
★ ★ ★
**EXCLUSIVE!
Handwriting Expert
Proves Farrah is
Howard Hughes**
★ ★ ★

JACKIE TO WED SELF

11. YOUR DEPRESSING HIT PARADE

Ever since Nero's original recording of "Arrivederchi Roma," to the recent rendition of "Heartbreak Hotel" by Leona Helmsley, history has been a long-playing album of one depressing hit after another. Here then, is a collection of classics that will stand forever in the annals of unpopular music. Memory makers of the past which are still sought after today, usually by customs agents.

#1 OH DONNA

  —Gary Hart

#2 I LEFT MY HEART IN SAN FRANCISCO

  —Dr. Barney Clark

#3 MICHELLE, MY BELLE

  —Lee Marvin

#4 BACK IN MY ARMS AGAIN

  —Venus de Milo

#5 REACH OUT AND I'LL BE THERE

  —J. Edgar Hoover

#6 WHERE THE BOYS ARE

  —Truman Capote

#7 I'VE GOT YOU UNDER MY SKIN

  —The Elephant Man

#8 A WHITER SHADE OF PALE

  —Michael Jackson

#9 HE AIN'T HEAVY (HE'S MY BROTHER)

  —Jimmy Carter

#10 HATS OFF TO LARRY

  —Moe & Curly

#11 LIGHT MY FIRE

  —Joan of Arc

#12 SUNNY

  —Claus van Bulow

#13 BRIDGE OVER TROUBLED WATERS

—Senator Ted Kennedy

#14 SILENCE IS GOLDEN

—G. Gordon Liddy

#15 I CAN SEE CLEARLY NOW

—Stevie Wonder

#16 ROSES ARE RED

—Senator Joe McCarthy

#17 PLEASE RELEASE ME, LET ME GO

—Sirhan Sirhan

#18 TWIST AND SHOUT

—Marquis de Sade

#19 LIFE COULD BE A DREAM

—Sigmund Freud

#20 DON'T IT MAKE MY BROWN EYES BLUE

—Dr. Joseph Mengele

PICKS OF THE WEEK

#1 OY TO THE WORLD

—Cretins Clearwater Revival

#2 IRAN, ALL THE WAY HOME

—Shah No No

#3 SERF CITY

—Bert Czar and the Rasputins

#4 INDIANA, HERE I COME

—Prince Charles

CLASSICAL FAVORITE

WALTZ OF THE CUSPIDORS

—Phil's Harmonic Orchestra

THE MOST DEPRESSING ALBUM OF ALL TIME!

GREATEST HITS OF '36

*—various Nazis. ***

SIDE ONE

#1 HATS OFF TO HEINRICH

#2 YOU ARE MEIN BLITZKREIG

#3 THE HEIDELBERG HOP

#4 FUËHRER OF THE PACK

#5 FIRST IT WAS ME, THEN IT WAS YOU, NOW IT'S V-2

#6 PLEASE, PLEASE, PLEASE, APPEASE ME

SIDE TWO

#1 SEALED WITH A STORM TROOPER

#2 NO TICKET TO RIDE

#3 SEE YOU IN STALINGRAD

#4 HEIL, HEIL, THE GANG'S ALL HERE

#5 I'M NOT THE ARYAN KIND

#6 WILL YOU SHOVE ME TOMORROW

*Here's how to order. Send your marks to "The House of Schmutz," Box 1936, Passaic, New Jersey. Remember, all records will be sent discreetly in a plain brown wrapper. But supplies are limited! So don't delay, order today, or your family will pay! Also available in CD (Certain Death).

12. BELIEVE IT OR DON'T OF DEPRESSION

Did you know that the amount of ex-stock brokers in one square mile of New York City outnumbers all the world's insects? Or that the legendary Szechuan chef Sam Chu, on his deathbed, requested that a funeral mask be fashioned from a side order of bean curd? Perhaps you didn't realize that the same man who designed the Trojan Horse, the Colossus of Rhodes and the Parthenon, Mike Moussaka, also built the Great Condo of Plato, and was subsequently treated for having an Edifice Complex.

Of course you didn't know, because it's taken years of painful research to uncover the most inhuman of oddities and the most unnatural of wonders, unbelievable stories, from places as far away and alien as Connecticut.

Yes, it's true. As you read about the Pygmy worms of Uganda who build immense mud homes with over three thousand chambers, many of which are rent-controlled, or of Ami Chumus, a Dervish who was forced to atone for his sins by placing a herring under his toupee, you will come away not only with a sense of fascination, but with feelings of disgust and nausea that will soon result in the most pitiful depths of depression.

Now, with this in mind, turn the page!

SOMEONE STANDING BENEATH A BUFFET TABLE IS 60 TIMES MORE LIKELY TO BE STRUCK BY A WAITER THAN BY LIGHTNING.

THE POLAROID THAT CRIED—
FOR ARGENTINA.

Juan Carlos Rodriguez, a male model and political dissident, was arrested the day the military took over his country — during a magazine shoot. Although Rodriguez has never been seen again, except in underwear ads at bus stops across Buenos Aires, the last polaroid taken of him has continued to weep for 17 years — **A MIRACLE THAT HAS BROUGHT THOUSANDS FROM AROUND THE WORLD WITH PERSONAL OFFERINGS— OF KLEENEX!**

MAHATMA FEINSTEIN, PH.D.

America's most successful therapist, can treat two neurotics simultaneously — **ON SEPARATE COUCHES!**

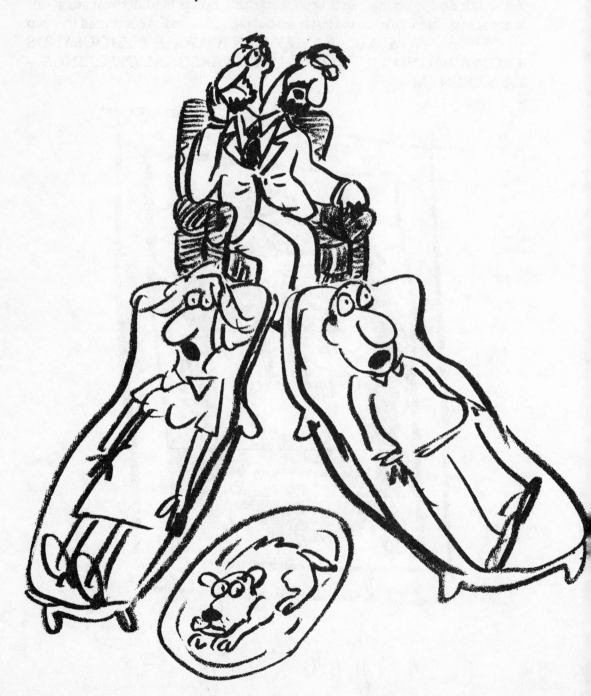

THE MAN WHO MADE MILLIONS— BEFORE HE WAS BORN!

While still a fetus, Ian de Placente became a Senior Editor at Shapolsky Publishing in Boston and, just a few months later, a Senior Vice-President. **ELECTED CHAIRMAN OF THE BOARD WHILE STILL NURSING**, he was given a plush corner crib. Finally, at the age of six months, de Placente decided to **THROW IN THE DIAPER** and turn over the reins of power to someone more infantile. **"YOU KNOW," HE SOBBED. "IT'S GONNA BE HARD TO WALK AWAY FROM THIS PLACE!"**

THE ZUCCHINI THAT COULD WRITE POETRY!

Was grown by Seymour Mendez of Barfville, West Virginia. It reached a length of 7 feet 4 inches, weighed 246 pounds — AND WAS EVENTU-ALLY NAMED IN A PATERNITY SUIT BY SOME TOMATO.

PREHISTORIC CAB DRIVER

North Dakota miners tunneling two miles underground unearthed the perfectly preserved body of a frozen neanderthal. Several days later **THE ICE-AGE SURVIVOR THAWED OUT** and, instinctively, trekked across the continent to a taxi garage in New York City where he was immediately put to work — **AFTER PRODUCING A STONE LICENSE!**

THE CIRCUMCISION THAT WAS CUT SHORT

Jacob Isaacson, an orthodox photographer specializing in circumcisions, **ACCIDENTALLY LET HIS CAMERA FLASH THE MOMENT THE TRADITIONAL JEWISH CEREMONY WAS BEING PERFORMED,** blinding the rabbi doing it, and turning the otherwise joyous occasion into one of tragic proportions. Ironically, only a few minutes before, Isaacson had quipped, **"IT WON'T BE LONG NOW!"**

NAT NABOB

A dentist from Oklahoma, can only pull teeth while sitting with his **BARE FEET IMMERSED IN ICE-COLD LAVORIS!**

POLYNESIAN BRIDGES

are made by mixing red clay and sand with **THE CRUSHED ORGANS OF TOLL COLLECTORS!**

THE CEO WHO SHEDS HIS SKIN LIKE A SNAKE!

Frank Serpentino, known for his ability to wriggle out of tough corporate situations, grows a new layer of skin **EVERY SIX MONTHS!** One associate, in 1956, made the mistake of asking, "Hey Frank, gimme some skin." — **AND HAS BEEN IN A STATE OF GLASSY-EYED SHOCK EVER SINCE!**

13. ANOREXIA: A GREAT WAY TO SLIM DOWN!

1.   2.   3.   4.   5.

> **"Eat, eat or you'll fall away to nothing."**
> —*author's Mother*.

Quite frequently, anorexics are so thin they're mistaken for doormats, hence the feeling that people are always walking all over them. In one instance Rozanne Leotardo, a dancer, lost over 317 pounds and became an imaginary point, a feat made even more extraordinary by the fact that she only weighed 104 pounds to begin with.

But that's not all the great news. Now Rozanne, no longer able to carry her weight at the ballet, has found love and happiness at MIT—inside an equation.

Like Rozanne, the Truly Depressed Person has to feel they have little or no substance, that's why the goal of this chapter is to reduce your daily caloric intake from about 1200 to around .000003. In this way, you'll shed all those trillions of body cells you really don't need and you'll learn to be content with just one cell, much like the amoeba, whose only drawback is a certain tendency to split — particularly when the check comes.

Therefore, what we have here is a rational, ordered plan for total starvation in less than a month. Sounds too good to be true, doesn't it? Actually, it's quite simple and it will effectively bring you the results you want in only 26 days.

Here's how it works: On Day #1 you eliminate all the foods that begin with the letter "A," such as avocados, acorn squash, and Aspergum. Day #2, you eliminate the "B's" and continue alphabetically until, on Day #26, you eliminate all the "Z's," such as zucchini, Zwieback and Zebra milk.

Study the following chart for suggestions and you will, in no time, reach incredible new heights of depression, although you probably won't have much depth.

DAY #1: ELIMINATE THE A's

Automat food, aardvark hearts, antediluvian chicken salad, ad hoc tomatoes, abstract enchiladas, auxiliary cowpeas.

DAY #2: ELIMINATE THE B's

Baboon fritters, badger balls, bellicose turnips, Bavarian beverages, broth (soup from a brothel), breast-fed clams, British food (contradiction in terms).

DAY #3: ELIMINATE THE C's

Counterfeit crab meat, corrugated fish, complex carbohydrates, Californian caviar, creme de mammoth, Caesarean salads.

DAY #4: ELIMINATE THE D's

Defective burgers, damn Yankee pot roast, dented quail, discounted drumsticks, Deviled Spam, Dead Sea bass, diesel oil and vinegar.

DAY #5: ELIMINATE THE E's

Embryonic mutton, erotic beets, eel taffy, evaporated gazelle milk, estrogen and tonic, embittered herbs, Edith Pilaf with mushrooms.

DAY #6: ELIMINATE THE F's

Felonious pastrami, fibroid meatballs, flame-broiled caribou, fifth helpings, Fallopian tubesteak, fluorescent foods (Three Mile Island cuisine).

DAY #7: ELIMINATE THE G's

Goldfish sticks, germicider, Garlic Toad Tamales, gangrene salads, grizzly pears, grudge brownies, guinea pig's feet.

DAY #8: ELIMINATE THE H's

Himalayan Jell-O, hypothetical pudding, Holiday cream of Penguin Soup, hairy halibut, Honey Glazed Squirrel, hawk and beans.

DAY #9: ELIMINATE THE I's

Iranian salami, incidental kippers, intangible malteds, infamous cream pies, Indian herring, inscrutable portions of nouvelle cuisine.

DAY #10: ELIMINATE THE J's

Jezebel peppers, Jersey cowpeas, junior high school wines, junkie lime pie, Japanese beetle bread, jellied beaver.

DAY #11: ELIMINATE THE K's

Kangaroo kasha, Kremlin ka-bobs, kvetch-up, key punch, knobby canta-loupe, kola crepes, kernels of Kentucky.

DAY #12: ELIMINATE THE L's

Leap frog's legs, Lebanese grits, laminated sausage, lacrosse buns, leopards in light tomato sauce, legal tenderloin, lewd prunes, Lobster cuspidor.

DAY #13: ELIMINATE THE M's

Manchurian candy dates, mail order meat, mule membranes, marinated mollusks, methanol milkshakes, Mekong mineral water.

DAY #14: ELIMINATE THE N's

Neo-tuna salad, Norwegian tamales, nebulous side-orders, nest egg foo young, nonabsorbent donuts, nonpartisan cheese.

DAY #15 ELIMINATE THE O's

Oklahoman escargot, oval celery, orangutan rump steaks, orthopedic quail, oxidized cookies, Oedipal sausages.

DAY #16 ELIMINATE THE P's

Pregnant anchovies, paraodoxial cuts of woodchucks, packaged newt, pachyderm wafers, pigeon pâté, pre-historic bean curd.

DAY #17 ELIMINATE THE Q's

Quiche with Lorraine on it, quadruplicate entrees, quarter horse radish, quarantine omelette (three eggs and a dash of smallpox virus).

DAY #18 ELIMINATE THE R's

Rabbit loaf, retrograde tacos, recycled plums, repellant sprouts, Rocky Mountain Spotted Peas, reconstructed oysters.

DAY #19 ELIMINATE THE S's

Shakespearean cutlets, sodium chloride, synthetic sturgeon, schnauzer dumplings, sacrificial lambs, Styrofoam toast, sun-dried Albanians, smoked tungsten.

DAY #20: ELIMINATE THE T's

Tasmanian Devil Dogs, tarnished cheese, thermonuclear chili, transparent beef, Tokyo Rose water, turkey brains.

DAY #21: ELIMINATE THE U's

Un-American cheese, umbilical cordeon bleu, Ugandan potato salad, upper crusts of bread, unsung hero sandwiches.

DAY #22: ELIMINATE THE V's

Vacuum-packed flamingos, Venusian ham, vibrating chives, Vitamin C-major, Vietnamese borscht, virulent strains of baby food.

DAY #23: ELIMINATE THE W's

Wandering jujubes, weightless derma, warm-blooded leeks, wed lox, walrus chowder, wildebeest croquettes, Wild Ass with Pesto Cream Sauce.

DAY #24: ELIMINATE THE X's

X-rated kumquats.

DAY #25: ELIMINATE THE Y's

Young blood pudding, yak fondue, Yugoslavian Cool Whip.

DAY #26: ELIMINATE THE Z's

Zambian soda bread, Ziplock mussels, zygote cheese, Zwieback of Notre Dame, zombie pollen.

14. THE MOST DEPRESSING TV COMMERCIALS

"OK. How about there's a fjord in your future?"

—one reason the author never got the
Norwegian Tourism account

In Minnesota, a steel worker is charged with attempting to drug a container of Parkay margarine with thorazine after it allegedly, during a private moment, whispered the word "butter" to him. In Tulsa, a schoolgirl is accused of trying to give Mr. Whipple a hernia transplant. And in Cincinnati, a couple is evicted from their apartment because they dared to use a roll-on in a way contrary to the laws of God and the FDA.

Far from being unrelated, these heinous crimes are only symptomatic of an even bigger and more bizarre plot—a concerted effort by America's largest advertising agencies to twist our deepest fears into skyrocketing sales for their thousands of worthless products and services.

But just don't thank the agencies, praise the Lord, although he probably won't get too much credit at the awards shows.

Yes today, the average person need look no further than his television screen to find commercials that are profoundly depressing. Therefore, as a stimulant to your eventual withdrawal from the human race, here are some of the most distressing 30 second spots of all time, each followed by a psychological analysis, so that you can understand exactly what subconscious syndromes they're playing upon.

COMMERCIAL #1

Shamefully, a middle-aged woman looks to her husband for compassion and understanding. He puts his arm around her and whispers, "Constipation?"

She nods and he immediately throws her down the stairs.

Next day, the kindly small town druggist perceives her problem before she can utter a single word.

"Feeling sluggish?"

She's too petrified to answer, since her body is in a cast.

Without hesitation he pulls a familiar blue bottle off the shelf and pours the contents through a slit in her face bandage. She appears to smile gratefully but is operated on later that week for the removal of an ingrown toilet seat.

ANALYSIS:

A serious demonstration of Constiphobia, or the crippling fear that your husband will run off with an unconstipated woman of twenty-seven.

COMMERCIAL #2

We open on a bare set. In walks an intense young man, conservatively dressed in a business suit, and carrying a thin leather attache case. He turns to the camera and speaks to us directly.

"I'm an investment banker with an aggressive portfolio and a net worth of 2.7 million dollars, but that's irrelevant. Because I'm here to talk to you, man to man. About a problem we all share. And about a product designed especially for us." He opens up his attache case and takes out an aerosol can.

"It's new A.D.S. — Anal Deodorant Spray. Nature's gentle lubricant for those warm, internal moments when just plain formaldehyde may not be enough. A.D.S. Made exclusively for today's backseat driver.

That's right. If you want him to be more of a man, try being more of a man yourself, with A.D.S. Remember, with A.D.S., you'll never be embarrassed to tell him, 'Kiss my assets.'"

ANALYSIS:

Obvious application of Anal/Oral Vexation, an irrepressible urge to brush one's teeth with Preparation H. (occasionally manifested by futile attempts to shrink hemorrhoids with Gleem).

COMMERCIAL #3

A yuppie in his early 30's bounds up the steps to embrace his eager wife. Angelically beaming, eyes closed, her upturned lips tremulously await his. He reaches for her but, suddenly, a green miasma billows from his mouth. She turns her head away in revulsion. No other words need be exchanged; the young man already knows it's the very same ghost that's haunted their marriage from the very beginning.

"Uncle Ernie?"

She nods and leads him to the bathroom.

There, under his wife's watchful eye, he attempts to exorcise the cloud of relative repugnance by gargling with the Bible, now in pleasant-tasting, liquid form.

Completely cleansed, the couple resume their affections, noting that the minty taste is a revelation.

ANALYSIS:

Classic example of Barfphobia, or the fear of vomiting on someone you love.

COMMERCIAL #4

And now we see a cowboy with lean, hard features set in an angular face, relaxing in a small circle of other prairie-wise men. It's twilight and it's obviously been a long cattle drive. Sprawled out, his back to a boulder, he warms himself by throwing a convenient junkie on the fire.

Tight shot of a familiar brand of cigarettes being passed around. Looking at their dusty, gritty hands, we immediately know that these men of the wilderness are fast running out of food, water, and Oil of Olay.

Finally, a close-up of a cowboy inhaling reflectively, with the unique look of satisfaction that can only be derived from doing one day's work while sitting home and collecting residuals for the rest of the year.

ANALYSIS:

Insipid use of Transvestophobia; the secret fear of being discovered doing Marlene Dietrich impressions in a mirrored jacuzzi while smoking a Virginia Slim.

But the list doesn't stop here. In Detroit a sectretary who couldn't decide what to wear, whether to go out or not, or if she should order red or white wine, was finally persuaded to buy "Ambivalence," a French fragrance designed especially for the woman who can't make up her mind.

And, in Tucson, a new breakfast cereal named Post-Mortem was test marketed and received an overwhelming response — from the city's large community of necrophiliacs. So don't fret, there are always fears and anxieties advertisers will employ to coerce your buying habits. Here are a final three:

AMERICAN EXPRESS IMPOTENCE

—performance failure, usually preceded by contact from a collection agency; curable only through tender, patient understanding, from Karl Malden.

TRIPOPHRENIA

—experienced as anxiety by those learning that the party punch they've been drinking is half LSD; usually followed by a frantic midnight search for a product that "consumes up to 47 times its weight in excess stomach acid."

DEFROCKOPHOBIA

—a nightmarish hallucination affecting priests; sever apprehension that friends and associates are secretly taunting, "Ring around the collar."

15. THE GREAT DEPRESSION 1929-41

It was the worst of times, therefore it was the best of times. It was the Great Depression. Twelve years in American history that helped bring a lot of people down — some about sixty stories.

This chapter will seek to briefly relive those golden days of economic turmoil by presenting some of the era's more significant facts and statistics in a brief chronology. But before we do, let us answer that most important of all questions. Could it happen again?

We should be so lucky.

1929

Stock Market crashes. The World Bank, the Bank of England and many Swiss banks all halt the practice of giving away free toasters.

1930

Financial markets in chaos. The DuPonts, Rockefellers and J. Paul Getty secretly meet to discuss the deepening crisis over lunch, at Burger King.

1931

Bond Market collapses. World unemployment almost equals the number of King Family Grandchildren.

1932

Great Dust Bowl. Steelers over Cowboys 31-17.

1933

Savings and Loan associations fail by the thousands. Rate of inflation swells to rival Sophie Tucker's blood pressure.

1934

Roosevelt meets with his top advisers and orders the New Deal. With a fresh deck.

1935

Leading Economic Indicators bleak. Gross National Product slacks off to three Budweisers and a pack of Tootsie Rolls.

1936

Price of gold plummets. Trading in blue chips replaced by trading in cow chips.

1937

Hollywood answers the call and attempts to lift the nation's spirits with the first musical starring bald actors, called "Broadway Follicles of 1937."

1938

Social turmoil. Riots at soup kitchens across the country due to emergency rationing of croutons.

1939

Money Supply hits all-time low. Security clearance from J. Edgar Hoover needed just to change a twenty.

1940

Trade deficit exceeds five trillion dollars. Secretary of the Treasury starts to learn shorthand.

1941

First signs of prosperity. Local men's shelters begin to go co-op.

16. SLOUCHING, SLUMPING AND DROOPING

BAD   GOOD

Few of us, if any, are born with the natural body language and the incomparable gait of a Quasimodo. We have to be taught. Yet this process is far from easy. Unfortunately, thanks to parental training early in life, we are often tempted to walk with our backs straight and our heads held high.

Taken to extremes, at parties or other social gatherings, you might unconsciously sit with your legs and arms uncrossed, which would inadvertently project the inner confidence of an untroubled mind.

This must be avoided at all costs. For it's just this kind of careless posturing that openly invites warm and intimate overtures from others.

Now, to evaluate precisely where you stand or crouch in these areas, the following visual test has been devised.

1. Does the position of her hands tell you that she's:
   a) shy
   b) promiscuous
   c) just had a nose job
   d) Lithuanian

2. The way he holds his cigarette reveals that he's:
   a) a swinger
   b) a nonsmoker
   c) a man who can be trusted
   d) an out-patient

3. Does the position of his head tell you that this man is:
   a) unhappy
   b) lonely
   c) a womanizer
   d) dead

4. Her body language would seem to indicate that she's:

    a) praying
    b) begging
    c) groveling
    d) looking for her contacts

5. This man is really telling us that:

    a) he's aloof
    b) he's secure
    c) he's insecure
    d) he has herpes

6. His facial expression discloses that he is most likely:
   a) frustrated
   b) defensive
   c) intimidated
   d) sexually involved with Margaret Thatcher

7. Does this man telegraph that he's:
   a) efficient
   b) ambitious
   c) helpless
   d) not good with hammers

8. **Her gestures immediately convey:**
    a) that she's nervous
    b) that she's uptight
    c) that she's furious
    d) that her mother is moving into the building

9. **From the physical relationship of this couple, would you say that this man is:**
    a) dominant
    b) submissive
    c) nearsighted
    d) hindsighted

10. **From her actions, would it seem that this woman is:**
   a) a good listener
   b) being supportive
   c) giving space
   d) about to make a point

ANSWERS: 1-c, 2-b or d, 3-a, b, or d. 4-d, 5-d, 6-d, 7-c or d, 8-a,b,c or d, 9-b or d, 10-d

To evaluate your lack of stature, total up the number of questions you answered correctly. Multiply this figure by 10. This will give you your score.

SCORE: If you got 65 or more points, then congratulate yourself, for you have the poise and bearing of a camel — with a hernia. Scores ranging from 33 to 64 indicate that you're still too erect. Come on, imagine that the weight of the world, or at least the weight of Willard Scott, is on your back. Last, and certainly least, if you scored 32 or below you have the grace and carriage of a high fashion model. No doubt, the possibility of you finding happiness as a flatworm, or even as vice-president, is virtually nil.

17. CHAIN-SMOKING, OBESITY, AND THE GOOD LIFE

(a hypnotic approach)

Allergies, migraines, phobias, guilt, insomnia, even if you've never suffered from any of them, there's still hope. How would you like to be able to sit in your dentist's chair and (by virtually using only your "will") feel every last drop of pain? Or how would you like to start smoking once and for all?

Well, there's no magic involved. Hypnosis is a powerful tool. One that can reach into our subconscious to conquer those deep-seated feelings of adequacy. Many times, the suggestions we give ourselves before going to sleep can help us to wake up totally exhausted.

It's no wonder that few tools, with the possible exception of a wrench applied to the forehead with pneumatic force, are as helpful in attaining a true state of depression as hypnosis.

Dr. Sven Galileo, the Italian hypnotist who was tortured by the Catholic church until he renounced his theory that he was the center of the universe, assures us that hypnosis has the power to make a profound change not only in our lives, but in our underwear as well. However, before he teaches us how to hypnotize ourselves, he recounts some of his more famous cases.

UNABLE TO GAIN WEIGHT

Margaret, a rather slender young cheerleader in her mid-seventies, came to me for help. As part of her treatment I asked her to bring me pictures of herself when she was obese. Naturally, she didn't have any, so I made her cut out the magazine photograph of an abnormally large woman and then made her affix it to the inside of her eyelids.

"In your mind's eye," I told her. "See yourself on Saturday night cruising all around town, uptown, downtown — propped up on a forklift." Well, suffice it to say, the negative self-imaging worked wonders and she reappeared at my office three months later with enough excess poundage to displace the Gulf of 'Aqaba.

UNABLE TO ACHIEVE FINANCIAL RUIN

One afternoon, a rather prosperous looking heart surgeon paid me a visit. But when I closed my office door, his cool and confident facade broke down completely and he confessed that despite the fact that he had a beautiful wife, two fine children and a lovely home, he was not a compulsive gambler.

Well, even I was shocked, but my years of professional training kept me from showing it. Within a few moments, I quickly induced a deep trance by reading him excerpts from Vanna White's life story. Then I suggested that he invest all his life savings in the New Guinea lottery.

It worked like a charm. Six weeks later he stopped by, on his way home from bankruptcy court, and announced that he was playing so much blackjack and poker that the only surgery he had time to perform were a few emergency bypass operations on hearts—you know, like the King of Hearts, Queen of Hearts, Jack of...

UNABLE TO DEVELOP A NICOTINE HABIT

Tom, a rather disturbed young man, entered my office one afternoon and proceeded to inform me that he had never touched a cigarette, except in 1976, when he had removed some butts that had been smoldering from inside his father's nose.

It was quite apparent that this incident had traumatized the young man quite severely, so I immediately put him into a deep trance by playing tapes of Michael Dukakis. While in the hypnotic state, I had him envision himself as a huge cigar being smoked simultaneously by Edward G. Robinson, Winston Churchill, Groucho Marx and Fidel Castro.

Although the treatment failed to make him a smoker, it did allow him to forgive his father and eventually achieve a workable relationship, with a wooden Indian.

DR. SVEN GALILEO'S TECHNIQUE FOR SELF-HYPNOSIS

First you need to fix your eyes on an object that will induce a hypnotic effect (a coin, a flickering flame, Raymond Burr on a swing) and concentrate. What you will start to notice is that your toupee is getting heavier and heavier. This is normal.

To take yourself a bit deeper into the state of hypnosis, imagine that you are standing at the top of an escalator. Start to count from ten to one as you go down. By the count of one you should be in the Boy's Wear department.

You're doing very well.

Now to enter the deepest levels of the trance, try to think of some place where you could relax and be happy (on a lake, a beach, a bed of cottage cheese). So far, so good. You are now ready to contact your subconscious, but don't call after 11:00 P.M.

ESTABLISHING COMMUNICATION WITH THE SUBCONSCIOUS

Communicating directly with the subconscious can pave the way for a real Inferiority Complex (or, in some cases, simplex). Here is an actual conversation that Mel O'Noma had with his subconscious id in order to find out why he feels compelled to yodel just before eating chicken nuggets.

MEL:

Who are you?

MEL'S ID:

Me.

MEL:

Me who?

MEL'S ID:

Medulla, you oblongata. Hey, that's a pretty good, huh, Boss.

MEL:

I need to know my deepest feelings. You have to let me see those early traumatic experiences that are making my life a neurotic mess.

MEL'S ID:

Yeah, yeah, sure. But wait, I gotta plenty good joke.

MEL:

Look, this is serious. This is my—

MEL'S ID:

OK, OK. What'dya get when you cross a Jewish American Princess with a computer?

MEL:

I give up.

MEL'S ID:

A computer that never goes down. Hey, Boss, thata one kills me!

MEL:

Maybe you don't understand. You're my subconscious mind and you have vital information locked away about my childhood. I've got to know what happened to me when I was eighteen months old.

MEL'S ID:

Holda your horses, I justa remember this one.

MEL:

Oh no.

MEL'S ID:

OK. When you cut Leonard Bernstein in half with a chainsaw, what'dya get?

MEL:

This is hopeless.

MEL'S ID:

A semiconductor. I love a that one too!

MEL:

Listen, you're my only chance. Stored away in your billions of grey cells and nerve endings are all those terrible events, things I've totally blocked out, that I can't remember, that are driving me crazy. Damn it! I can't wait another second, do you hear me!?

MEL'S ID:

Hey, boss, now I gotta one thata kills me!

MEL:

 Please...

MEL'S ID:

If someone who's half Viking and half Turkish dies, where a they go?

MEL:

No more, please.

MEL'S ID:

Valhalvah!! Hey, you gotta admit, thatsa the best one yet, huh Boss. Boss?

From these dialogues with his subconscious id, Mel learned that in the great supermarket of life, he was standing on the express checkout line. OK. You are now ready to learn a new hypnotic technique, one developed by General Motors.

THE POWER OF AUTO SUGGESTION

Lie down in a comfortable position. Using the techniques for self-hypnosis you've just been given, put yourself into a deep trance. Now see yourself in a powerful Ferrari winding up and down scenic roads in the south of France. Feel the freedom and exhilaration as you let out the throttle.

Faster and faster, there's nothing on earth that can stop you. Now you're flying, flying — unfortunately off a cliff — and suddenly you're scattered all over the hillside, a twisted mass of burning metal. OK. Slowly bring yourself out of the trance and, for the rest of the day, experience the feeling of being a total wreck.

OTHER SPECIAL USES FOR HYPNOSIS

1. DISLEARNING A LANGUAGE

By playing a special blank cassette before going to sleep, you can reduce your verbal repertoire to a series of grunts, groans, and Tom Jones imitations.

2. INCREASING STRESS

The aim here is to impart the continual feeling, through hypnotic imagery, that Orson Welles is sitting on your chest.

3. GETTING MIGRAINES

Concentrate on a flickering candle. Now envision that the top of your head has been spot-welded to a Kawasaki 750.

18. MONOTONY: THE BORED GAME FOR THE WHOLE FAMILY

Back in the 30's a wonderful board game was created that reflected the colorful locales of Atlantic City, New Jersey. For generations, it's amused millions of people around the world and has sparked, in friends and family alike, involvement, controversy but most of all good, clean fun. Small wonder it should be avoided at all costs.

The Truly Depressed Person needs a new type of game that addresses who he or she is. A game that will capture his or her lack of interest and disinvolvement with reality. Fortunately, Monotony provides exactly what the Truly Depressed person has been looking for, under the bed. It resembles that other game except that there are certain substitutions, such as "Park Bench" for "Park Place." Likewise, there are "No Chance" and "Community Rest" cards.

All right. Here's how you don't play.

THE RULES OF MONOTONY

1. To start, all players go directly to Jail.

2. They go directly to jail.

3. They do not pass Go.

4. They do not collect $200, they just rot.

5. To get out of Jail, players must take turns trying to roll an even.

6. This is unlikely, since both dice are blank.

7. As the game continues, players should take turns going nowhere.

8. No money is traded.

9. No houses or hotels built.

10. No property exchanged.

11. No deals made.

12. And the player who goes to sleep first, wins.

19.
The National Enema
"America's Most Depressing Paper" (Vol. II)

CONCLUSIVE NEW EVIDENCE PROVES
DONNY OSMOND
DID NOT KILL JFK

Beauty Tips from Leon Spinks

★ ★ ★

Jimmy Hoffa: How I Spent My Summer Vacation

★ ★ ★

Secrets the FBI, CIA, and Connie Francis Knew, But Never Told Us

Body Language Expert Says Billy Graham is Jewish

★ ★ ★

Three out of Four Don't Know Who Seymour Rodriguez Is

★ ★ ★

How Expectant Mothers Threaten America's Survival

HITLER PLEADS: LET'S BURY MY PAST

20. ANTIDEPRESSANTS: THE COMPLETE LOWDOWN

The growing body of scientific evidence, including the obese body of one lab assistant in Topeka, all seem to warn of the grave dangers associated with antidepressant drugs, the most disconcerting of which is that they all tend to prevent depression.

Indeed, many of these medications are notorious for causing dizziness, lightheadedness and a loss of balance, particularly in one's checking account.

In severe cases, we have seen these very same drugs produce extreme agitation, impaired vision and dry mouth, not unlike those symptoms observed in guests on the Morton Downey show.

What's more, even European scientists have reported disturbing results. Researchers at the Sorbonne (using only 5 mgs of Elavil and a copy of Penthouse) were able to induce heat rash in a penguin.

Unfortunately, despite the crushing weight of all this medical evidence, there are still some individuals who will insist on taking these medications. For them, we have prepared the following questions and answers.

Q. What are the long-term side effects of antidepressive drugs?

A. Many doctors are concerned about the unpleasant effects that these drugs can have over a long period of time. In a series of incidents reported in Des Moines, the constant use of these medications provoked a continuous urge to whistle, especially in those with no lips.

Q. What is the success rate of antidepressive drugs?

A. Remarkably high. In fact, many people who undergo this kind of medical treatment become normal, healthy, functioning human beings for the rest of their lives, or till the end of the week, whichever comes first.

Q. Will an antidepressive drug alter my sex life?

A. Not if you're not having one. But for many men, antidepressive drugs cause a decline in sexuality so severe that the resultant sperm count can often be measured on the fingers of just one hand, usually the right.

Q. Antidepressive medicines have not been successful in treating my depression. What should I do?

A. Thank your lucky stars. Fortunately, no treatment is 100% effective, so go out and celebrate. By this time next year you should be ready to spend all your days and nights in Paris, that is, more specifically, plaster of Paris.

Q. What should I do if a particular medication makes me sleepy?

A. Sleep.

IMPORTANT!

Study the following chart carefully. It details the major side effects of the leading antidepressive drugs as detailed by the AMA (American Mandolin Association).

ANTI-DEPRESSANT	DOSAGE	MAJOR SIDE EFFECTS
1. Elavil	2 tons	Triggers anti-Semitism in clams; may cause oysters to become bedridden.
2. Phelantin	5 quarts	Evokes an irrepressible need to fondle George Bush.
3. Sinequan	10,000 mgs	Instrumental in inspiring Breakdown dancing (form of break dancing where you stand on a corner and have an anxiety attack).
4. Nardil	7 tsp	Brings on homosexuality in paramecium; may cause TV anchormen to have occasional insights.
5. Dilantin	7 kegs	Will produce sterility in life-insurance salesmen.*
6. Pertofrane	9 mugs	Suspected of causing jowls in Cornish hens; may provoke Armenians to go ice fishing, often catching a few cubes.
7. Triavi	11 kilos	Motivates carpenters to join splinter groups; associated with the high incidence of swollen ankles among streetwalkers.
8. Aventyl	.05 barrels	Shown to be the major cause of ulcers in caribou; plus hemorrhoids in sperm whales.
9. Vivactil	.005 bushels	Said to produce shakiness and slurred or garbled speech in fans of Rocky I, II and III.
10. Parnatel	44 magnums	Has been linked to retarded ejaculation in Certified Public Accountants.

*Although some medical opinion contends this is beneficial.

21. MOROSE THE CAT
(DEPRESSED PET OF THE YEAR)

22. HOW TO LOSE MONEY DURING THE COMING GOOD YEARS

> "It is never too late to invest in your financial insecurity."
>
> —*E.F. Glutton*

Because emotional and monetary collapse often go hand in hand, this chapter will supply you with the basic tenets of downside economics. To accomplish this, we will draw upon the resources and experience of **ENTREPRENEUTER** ("The Magazine For Eunuchs Who Mean Business").

Through the years, this remarkable publication has annually listed the companies in the Misfortune 500 and has covered an extraordinary number of up-to-the-minutes stories, some of which you may recall:

THE $100 BILLION ENERGY QUESTION: WILL AMERICA BE ABLE TO EXTRACT CRUDE OIL FROM DON RICKLES?

☆ ☆ ☆

HOW TO DEVELOP THE EXTRAORDINARY "WILL TO LOSE"

☆ ☆ ☆

CO-OP CONVERSION IN ZIMBABWE

☆ ☆ ☆

ITT LINKED TO BUSINESS COMMUNITY, CLAIMS TOP MAFIA INFORMER

☆ ☆ ☆

MOSHE DAYAN: HOW I SAVE UP TO 50% ON CONTACT LENSES

☆ ☆ ☆

YOUNG SUICIDE OF THE MONTH

☆ ☆ ☆

Plus **ENTREPRENEUTER** was the first to report that:

CAL TECH SCIENTISTS DISCOVER NUCLEAR POTENTIAL IN ALL-BRAN!

In the following excerpts, we will cull some of the finest information published in the pages of **ENTREPRENEUTER** in the sincere hope that you'll never trade in your pacifier for the true challenges of life.

WHY YOU SHOULD APPLY FOR A DISCREDIT CARD
(First appeared, 6/83)

Practically anyone can get Master Charge; that's why **ENTREPRENEU-TER** recommends a totally new kind of financial instrument: SLAVE CHARGE— The First Credit Card for Masochists.

It gives anyone, even total strangers, the right to command you to put their purchases on your card. From a pair of sweat socks to a mink coat all the way up to a Mercedes Benz, SLAVE CHARGE is the preferred way to create an unbalanced budget, and therefore an unbalanced mind.

Not a Gold Card, not a Green Card, SLAVE CHARGE is made of genuine tin, which immediately conveys an incredible lack of status whenever you're ordered to present it. Now look at these disadvantages!

NO CREDIT LIMIT

Why should there be? The deeper and deeper you sink into debt, the deeper you'll be sinking into depression.

HIGH ANNUAL FEES

Annual membership for your personalized SLAVE CHARGE is just under $160 million, only about half the cost of a B-1 bomber.

FREE CZECHS

Unlimited access to your home is guaranteed to all refugees from Prague.

CREDIT CARD PROTECTION

Each and every SLAVE CHARGE card comes with a prefitted condom.

DEFERRED CUSTOMER SERVICE

Just dial 1-800-KISS OFF and be completely assured of a continuous busy signal.

LOSS OR THEFT?

Not to worry. Should your card ever be lost or stolen, you're only responsible for everything over $50.00. Now what could be simpler?

DISMEMBERSHIP HAS ITS PRIVILEGES

Of course, substantial penalties for missing monthly payments may be imposed that will, quite literally, cost you an arm and a leg.

You are hereby ordered to request your SLAVE CHARGE today. Come on. Get the discredit you deserve.

HIGH RISK/NO GAIN BUSINESS OPPORTUNITIES
(8/86 issue, regular feature)

Within six months, Harvey Bash of Toledo, Ohio, with start-up capital of only $6,000,000, was reduced to crooning "Moon River" at a local men's shelter. All by investing in a peanut butter company that had as its advertising theme: *TASTES SO GOOD YOU'LL WANNA KISS OUR NUTS!*

Within three months, Thelma Periodonto, through careful money mismanagement, was able to move from being "Head of Production" at a large company to being "Head of Lettuce." This, just by investing her life savings in a school that specialized in giving Charleston lessons to Navajos.

And finally, Senator Daniel Patrick Moribund found, after following our advice, that not only couldn't he get a new lease on life, he couldn't even get a sublet.

Of course, while these stories of ruin, failure and industrial-strength migraines are highly inspirational, it is better not to expect too little too soon.

Therefore, in order to maximize your risk, divide your funds evenly among the following investments:

1. Open up a Hebrew National frankfurter stand on the Iraqi/Iranian border.

2. Become a consultant in the highly lucrative sombrero rental field.

3. Invest in a ski-lift at the base of Mount St. Helens.

4. Start a spiritual resumé service that specializes in giving people's past life experience.*

5. Use the remainder of your funds to produce a definitive recording of "Ain't We Got Fun" in Gaelic.

6. Franchise a chain of Joel Steinberg day-care centers.

7. Manage a new restaurant featuring acupuncture, where patrons get stuck with the check**.

8. Finance a major motion picture about auto racing and necrophilia, called "Dead Heat".

9. Become a professional impersonator who only does imitations of John Glenn.

10. Buy Savings Bonds — in El Salvador.

THE UNREAL ESTATE SECTION
OUTER MONGOLIA
(Unspoiled Mountain Retreat)

Surrounded by breathtaking views, beautiful streams and hordes of Chinese communists, these 500 inaccessible acres are a dream come true. Lush grass, virgin timber, trout fishing and Soviet troops, all practically on your doorstep. Hunt deer, elk and coolies. Snowmobile through scenic avalanches. A very unique retreat yet, less than five minutes away, you can always enjoy the latest restaurants, movies and purges. Price 6.89 yen ($10,857,913.03).

IMPORTANT!

ENTREPRENEUTER magazine considers its sources totally unreliable and verifies no data what-so-ever; although reporting accuracies may occur, subsequently, any reader using this information does so with the understanding that, on rare occasions, a profit may be accidently generated.

No part of ENTREPRENEUTER may be reproduced or transmitted in any form by any means without the written permission of the publisher, if you can find him in Argentina.

*Actually, in California, this could work.
**Actually, in California, this could work too.

23. THE DEPRESSED READING LIST

As an erudite and highly perceptive shut-in, it is very important for you to be cognizant of the latest and most profound works in the field of depressive literature, such as "The Importance of Being Ernest Borgnine," by Ernest Borgnine.

Indeed, the Truly Depressed Person should have an almost encyclopedic knowledge of these books which can easily be acquired by consulting "The Reader's Guide to Periodical Depression." A copy of Roget's Thesaurus might also be helpful, but if he's not home, try stealing someone else's.

IMPORTANT: Try to obtain your favorite publisher's blacklist, however, if you can't, settle for his backhand.

With this in mind, here are a number of volumes, each one selected exclusively for your reading displeasure:

1. FORESKIN AND SEVEN YEARS AGO

—the memoirs of a Lincolnesque rabbi.

2. ANXIETY WITHOUT FEAR

—a famous psychologist explains how she lives in terror 24 hours a day — and loves it!

3. THE WORLD'S GREATEST CRASH DIET

—finger lickin' good recipes from the Andes survivors.

4. THE CARPETBUGGERS

—a sizzling saga of sex and passion, set against the lusty background of a remnants sale.

5. THE PRIMAL PODIATRIST

—new vistas in the treatment of callused souls.

6. THE TURKEY IN THE RYE

—the long awaited novel from J.D.L. Salazar.

7. FOR YOUR EYES ONLY

—he had a license to kill...and practice optometry.

8. LIVE SHORTER NOW

—748 delightful treats, all made from salt, sugar, caffeine, and recycled eggs.

9. THE ART OF LOATHING

—intolerance, bigotry, persecution—true, they're noble concepts, but how do we implement them in our daily lives? A thought-provoking work by R.D. Fang.

10. THE ORIGIN OF THE FECES

—the controversial new book by a Darwinian proctologist.

11. FOR WHOM THE BELL TOLLS

—it tolls for thee, especially on long-distance calls.

12. THE BOOK OF LISPS

—superbly entertaining and informative, the one the critics have been talking about: 687 intriguing pages chockful of cleft palates.

13. DELMONTE'S INFERNO*

—a noted theologian asserts that eating canned vegetables will damn one for eternity and insists that repentance is only valid when offered, on one's knees, before a fresh salad bar. By the celebrated author of "Methodist Acting."

14. THE JOY OF BEING A SINGLE VEGETARIAN

—at last! The book that shows you how to tell the fruits from the vegetables.

15. STRICT FREUDIANS

—they get their kicks out of tying their patients to the couch.

16. FRIDAY, THE RABBI ATE A SHISKA

(no explanation necessary)

24. DEPRESSIONS IN THE EARTH

1. Ravines
2. Craters
3. Gullies
4. Valleys
5. Fjords
6. Ruts
7. Crevices
8. Cracks
9. Faults
10. Gorges
11. Canyons
12. Glens
13. Abysses
14. Gulfs
15. Chasms
16. Caverns
17. Pits
18. Shafts
19. Hollows
20. Wells
21. Newark, New Jersey
22. Fissures
23. Dales
24. Dells
25. Dingles
26. Gaps
27. Gulches
28. Gullys
29. Notches
30. Straths

25.
The National Enema
"America's Most Depressing Paper" (Vol. III)

TOP SCIENTIST BLAMES WEATHER FOR AMERICA'S BITTER-COLD WINTER

Amazing New Drug Offers Hope for Millions Crippled by Lawrence Welk

★ ★ ★

Luther Burbank Talks About His "Roots"

★ ★ ★

79% Favor Transplanting Organs of Prince Charles

U.S. Air Force Jet Flies into Cloud—And Tiny Tim Comes Out!

★ ★ ★

Gov't Claims Tap Dancing Linked to Cancer

★ ★ ★

Top Sex Researcher Says Most American Men Lose Viginity after Intercourse

RICHARD NIXON REVEALS SECRET AFFAIR—WITH HIS WIFE!

26. DARKNESS, DINGINESS, AND OTHER DECORATING TIPS

> "Home is where the heart is...and liver...and kidneys..."
>
> —*Psychopathic Butcher*

Deciding on a Truly Depressing decor, one that reflects ourselves as well as repels others, can be quite a major undertaking. Those environments where we eat and sleep, wonder and dream, love and raise a family, should feel less like a personal statement and more like solitary.

To that end, this chapter will concern itself with turning those otherwise bright and cheery apartments dark and dreary. Even those with the natural drawbacks of twenty-foot ceilings, skylights and working fireplaces can be made to feel much more like broom closets. OK. Answer these three questions:

1. Do bay windows make you nauseous?

2. Does a stone fireplace centrally located leave you disoriented?

3. Is a cozy living room enough to put you on the critical list?

If you answered "yes" to any or all of these questions, then you may have talent as an **INFERIOR DECORATOR** (now don't be modest!). But to find out how much, study the illustration below.

LIST THE 15 THINGS WRONG WITH THIS PICTURE!!

ANSWERS

1. Cocker spaniel doesn't have mites.

2. Upstairs toilet not overflowing.

3. Windows, with southern exposure, not bricked up.

4. Antique pine hutch upright.

5. Classical glass coffee table inspires too much conversational ease.

6. Blue and white English saucers not being used as Frisbees.

7. Tropical fish, in wall-sunken aquarium, not being fed Drano.

8. Biscuit-colored rug by hearth, not smoldering.

9. Furry white throw pillows have no pepperoni stains.

10. Cat not choking on fur balls.

11. Floor-to-ceiling Georgian mirror not shattered.

12. Solarian floor tiles not buckling.

13. Viennese Sewing Cabinet (from the 18th century) has no bullet holes.

14. Roaches not breeding under cornice molding.

15. Children not mounted over fireplace.

Even if you, like most Americans, were able to identify all fifteen, there's still much to be learned about getting pipes to rust, mold to grow, paint to peel, plaster to fall, dust to build, and termites to infest. That's why we've invited the country's foremost Inferior Decorator to answer your questions.

ASK MR. NIX-IT

Dear Mr. Nix-It:

My kitchen is light. Very light. The entire room has white paneling and Formica surfaces. There are four large bay windows in each wall. What can I do, inexpensively if possible, to darken up this room and make it feel smaller?

Sincerely,
Barbara B.
White House, Washington, D.C.

Dear Barbara:

Much of the lightheartedness of your kitchen comes from the paneling and formica surface. I would propose tarring these over. But often the hardest part of remodeling one's kitchen is trying to envision what the final results will be. The "Junkyard Designer Kit" offers literally hundreds of items—from old tires to aging bran muffins—that can all be used to cut down on that annoying feeling of spaciousness. As for the windows, try simple lace curtains. While characteristic of Swedish interiors, you can dress them up with the entrails of Democrats.

Dear Mr. Nix-it:

My problem is this. Although I always make sure to keep them out of the light, while also not giving them any water whatsoever, my petunias and sunflowers are thriving like there's no tomorrow. Is there anything I can do to stop all this crazy growth?

Very truly yours,
Mean Thumb
Wichita Falls

Dear Mean Thumb:

Your letter didn't specify if you were male or female, so I'm assuming you're neither. Anyway, the problem could be that you're inadvertently talking to your plants. Try reading to them instead. The works of Jacqueline Susann, plays by Ibsen, Nixon's memoirs, all have been shown to have a withering effect.

☜   ☜   ☜

Dear Mr. Nix-It:

The upstairs bathroom of our two story split-level ranch house has unevenly slanted dormer walls and poor insulation. This is just fine. My real problem is that, very recently, my toilet has started to flush perfectly and will no longer stop up and overflow. Suffice to say, I am a real novice at clogging pipes and drains. Can you give me some helpful hints?

Thanks a lot,
Will Knot
Portland, Oregon

☜   ☜   ☜

Dear Will:

Although it's not common knowledge, you can stuff up a toilet simply by removing a pipe or two. Or by taking a circus pinhead and inverting him upside down in the bowl. In addition, even the most modest home has patchwork quilts, high tea tables, ginger-jar lamps, armoires and even bird prints, all of which can be flushed to achieve exactly the same kind of results. I remember, as a child growing up, that my mother and aunt always kept cheddar cheese in their bathrooms, the point of which escapes me.

☜   ☜   ☜

Dear Mr. Nix-It:

Our living room is exceptionally long and wide. The walls are knotty pine, the ceiling beams are a rich, stained walnut and the draperies have a chestnut antique color. Frankly, my wife and I are heartsick over the warmth and comfort this room offers our family. Can you sketch an arrangement that will make this area colder and less inviting?

> The Kleevers
> 26 Beaver Lane
> Beverly Hills, CA

Dear Mr. & Mrs. Kleever:

A home should reflect the artistry of a bygone era, though not later than the Pleistocene epoch. First, try surrounding yourself with antiques. I would suggest a synthesis of Victorian dressing tables, floral fabrics, a family of Bedouins, and some eighteenth century oils. But remember, the most important thing is not to be intimidated by the magnitude of the job itself. A lot of people, much like yourself, know exactly what they want, but have no experience with flamethrowers.

27. DRESSING FOR DEPRESSION (OR THE SCHLEPPIE HANDBOOK)

When it comes to dressing, creating a good first depression is very important. Materials such as cotton, linen and silk should be avoided at all costs in favor of the more traditional canvas and burlap.

Wherever you go, men wonder about the pros and cons of diamond stickpins. It's safe to say that these are appropriate on certain occasions, but only when worn through the nose. Also, never underestimate the value of a sharp crease, particularly when it's running down the side of your body and not the suit.

Amazingly, few people realize what an incredible impact their clothing has, especially if they haven't changed their underwear in several years. It can make the crucial difference in whether others treat you with respect, reverence or methadone.

Yes, it's true. Through the proper combination of styles and colors, you can command your special place in the sun, right out there on top of a storm sewer.

In a now-famous set of experiments, twelve men were sent to the Four Seasons, one of New York's most expensive and exclusive restaurants. Six of the twelve were given custom-fitted Italian suits, Gucci shoes and imported silk ties to wear. The other six were given overalls, linoleum shoes, and imported silkworms to wear.

Well, suffice to say, all six of the first group were immediately seated by the maitre d', but only four of the second, so the conclusions are pretty apparent.

GENTLEMAN'S DRAWN AND QUARTERLY

Unfortunately, this type of expert fashion consultation is not available to the general public. That's why "Gentleman's Drawn and Quarterly" is an excellent magazine for the Truly Depressed, since not only does it provide the latest, up-to-the-minute looks in complete degradation, but it can also be slept on.

Recently, they ran a special feature on the depressed dress code for California. From San Diego to San Francisco, floral strait jackets with wide lapels were suggested, as well as ties and lightweight sweaters woven from a blend of natural cotton and tofu.

However, in the Northeast, this kind of laid-back approach is often frowned upon. Especially by Emil of Flatbush, a fashion designer associated with Brooklyn Brothers, a burnt-out department store situated near the Manhattan bridge. Emil notes that the average depressed man, even in this day and age, does not know the fundamentals about dressing shabbily.

ADVICE FROM "EMIL OF FLATBUSH"

"There are a number of ways to overcome the advantages of a suit that looks like a million," says Emil. "If the pants fit you properly in the crotch, politely ask two construction workers to pretend you're a wishbone. Similarly, if you have accidentally tied a full Windsor, see if you can locate some Klansmen who can help you with a more practical hangman's knot.

In conclusion, pinstripes should be avoided at all costs, though prison stripes are acceptable and, if you really get lucky, the city will come along and paint a stripe down the center of your forehead."

OK, what you really need at this point is a frame of reference to help give your sartorial style the disheveled edge:

NOT ACCEPTABLE	ACCEPTABLE
Cotton sweaters	Steel-wool sweaters
Wing-tipped shoes	Chicken wing-tipped shoes
Pockets in shirt	Pockets in face
Oxford cloth shirt	Tablecloth shirt
Ascot ties	Mascot ties
Gucci shoes	Horseshoes
Turtleneck sweater	Turtle-soup sweater
Camel's hair coat	Pubic hair coat

POLLY AND ESTHER PUT IT ALL IN PERSPECTIVE

Despite the current hoopla, fashion has existed in many cultures over thousands of years. Polly and Esther, two Siamese historians, point to the fact that certain headhunting tribes of Northern Samalia are forbidden, during large sit down dinners, to wear paisley ties.

What's more, during the Triassic period, prehistoric designers ruled the earth, including Calvin Groc, who died prematurely while trying to explain the concept of a preshrunk loin cloth to an irate neanderthal.

Finally, the two historians contend, the Lord of Abraham did not smite all of Egypt's first born before offering them a choice; as a matter of fact, initially, he gave them the option of just having to wear plaid brown sports jackets.

28. JACK MEDOFF'S REAL LIFE DEPRESSION

"I'm afraid we're going to have to let you go, Perkins."

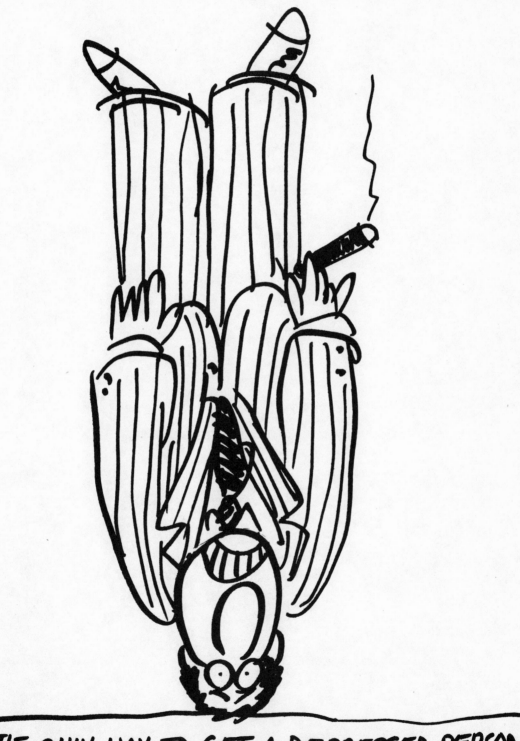

THE ONLY WAY TO GET A DEPRESSED PERSON
TO SMILE IS TO DRAW THEM UPSIDE DOWN.

29. THE THRILL OF DEFEAT (AND THE AGONY OF VICTORY)

> "Losing isn't everything. It's the only thing!"
>
> —*Coach Wince Lumbago*

So says one of the great ones. An inspiration to us all, Coach Lumbago, himself a former receiver, still holds the NFL record (10,693) for the most times force-fed Astroturf in a single season.

In the spirit of his memory (he died tragically when the Pittsburgh Steelers accidentally tap danced across his trachea) this chapter will recount the achievements of other world-class champions. Each should serve as a compelling reminder to the Truly Depressed. Proof positive that it is never (NEVER!) too late to snatch defeat from the jaws of victory.

Of course, unlike more famous athletes like Joe Namath, Mickey Mantle and Schlomo Rodriguez, these unsung heros often compete in events of which we've heard little or nothing about. To correct this injustice, we've provided a list of some of the most depressing events in sports history.

SKYBARFING

The greatest altitude at which a skydiver has ever felt nauseous was achieved by Perry Stalsis on July 31st, 1972, when he puked at 41,000 feet after realizing that he had forgotten his parachute.

THE U.S. OPEN FLY GOLF TOURNAMENT

On May 23rd, 1967, Sam Peed became the only man to shoot 269 over 72 holes, without once having closed his zipper.

SHORTEST TITLE BOUT

On September 5th, 1923, a capacity crowd filled Yankee Stadium to witness Peewee Berman (2'5") and Midge Speck (1'11") fight it out to be the undisputed Paperweight Champion of the World. However, in the unprecedented seventh round, both fighters were simultaneously KO'd when the referee accidentally stepped on them.

SLOWEST 5000 METERS

18 year old Hans Metternich of Austria, in the 1932 Los Angeles Olympics, set a record of 57 years, 45 days, 11 hours, 12 minutes and 55 seconds, long enough for him to obtain American citizenship and retire on Social Security, just before crossing the finish line.

POLE VAULTING

Lech Walesa leapt a record 75'6" trying to escape from police in his native Warsaw, the highest mark ever set by a Pole.

25% OFF SAILING

On July 18th, 1981, yachts belonging to J.C. Penney's, Macy's, and Bloomingdales' all competed in the first Retail Regatta to be held in New York Harbor. Skippers for all three vessels, however, were disqualified following allegations that their times were drastically marked down.

A U.S. FOUR MAN BOOBSLED TEAM

Led by Iggy Norant, would have easily taken the world championship at Lake Flaccid, New York, had it not been August.

BASEBALL'S 22ND ANNUAL ALL-SITAR GAME

Was played in New Dehli on April 23rd, 1982. The New York Frets lost 89-0 after being completely mystified by a series of strange pitches, none of which seemed to exist in Western music.

THE MASTERS AND JOHNSON'S GOLF TOURNAMENT

Was lost by Harold Palmer on the final hole when, before a gallery of thousands, he was unable to bring his wife Birdie to climax, even though she was only one stroke away.

SINGLE'S TENNIS

On October 3rd, 1985, the women's title was again captured by Gertrude Cohen of Westhampton, Long Island, who has played for 87 years without a partner.

THE 103RD FREAKNESS STAKES

Was won by Infirmed, a horse with three legs and two heads. The jockey was Grover Tesque.

THE 1988 NRA (NATIONAL RIBALD ASSOCIATION) HUNTING TROPHY

Went to Flem Spittle for killing a record 438 deer all in one day — with his sense of humor.

WORLD SIX-FIGURE SKATING CHAMPIONSHIP

In Vienna, on April 15th, 1983, Yvonne Googolplex, a previously un-known accountant, skated away with the title after flawlessly executing eight flying leaps, three midair somersaults and a backwards split, all while embez-zling $863,217 from her employer.

THE U.S. PRAWN TENNIS ASSOCIATION

On May 26, 1977, defending champion Sam "Wok Around the Clock" Chow relentlessly battered his longtime adversary Sidney Wu in straight sets, before deep-frying him.

THE STANLEY AND LIVINGSTON CUP

Special NHL trophy in the shape of Bill Murray; awarded to explorers who greet lost doctors in the jungle by saying, "You're a hockey puck, I presume?" Presented to the family of Wayne Zetzsky, in 1985.

NUMBERS RACKETBALL

Present champion Nicky "The Enforcer" Spumoni of Hoboken retained his present title when he crushed Vinny "The Cubist" Albano, in a grudge match, by serving sixteen consecutive wrecking balls.

A FINAL DEPRESSING CHALLENGE!

Yet, there are some immortals who require no explanation. So, as a World Class Loser, you should have no trouble whatsoever identifying them from the records they've set.

CAN YOU NAME

1. The pitcher who holds the American League record for consecutive strikeouts — in singles bars?

2. The only three-time world heavyweight champion to have his poetic license revoked in the state of New Jersey?

3. The basketball player who has accumulated the greatest number of personal fouls for double dribbling, from either side of his mouth?

4. The boy wonder from Toledo who, at the age of eleven, has bowled 183 perfect (300-point) games with a severed head?

5. The NHL goalie who has spent a total of 637 minutes in the penalty box for attempting to stuff Howard Cosell with crabmeat?

(ANSWERS BELOW)

1. Whitey Foo, New York Yangtzes

2. Salvador Ali

3. Milt Chambermaid, L.A. Quakers

4. Gilbert "Gil" O' Tene

5. Wilson Puckett, Montreal Rumanians

30. STAYING IN BED: THE BEST EXERCISE

The secret of total lethargy is as easy as lying down. You can siesta on a brass bed, a berth, or if you're a woman, a Bertha. It really doesn't matter so long as you never get up. In fact, total depression requires that you never leave your bed, except in cases of extreme emergency, such as fire, earthquake, or getting another box of Cheese Doodles.

Remember, your dreams of becoming a Truly Depressed Person can come true if you always keep this in mind: the earlier you rise, the earlier you can go back to sleep. Now here are some helpful hints:

TYPES OF BEDS

1. Water bed
2. Sea bed
3. Bed of lettuce
4. Convertible sofa
5. Sofa that refuses to convert

AIDS TO SLEEPING

1. Ted Koppel
2. Tortoni sedative
3. Milk of Amnesia
4. Industrial-strength orgasm
5. Chevy dropped obliquely on bridge of nose

HINDRANCES TO SLEEPING

1. Drippy spouse
2. Coyotes in foyer
3. Sandpaper massage
4. Arousal attempt by Telly Savalas
5. Upstairs neighbor practicing three-hour tap dance based on "War and Peace."

THE TWO BEST PLACES TO SLEEP

1. On a park bench
2. On a park wench

24 HOUR SLEEP SCHEDULE

MORNING

7:30 Alarm goes off
7:31 Alarm hits jogger
8:42 Take catnap
8:43 Cat takes it back
10:54 Eyes get heavy
10:57 Eyes go on diet
11:02 Fall into arms of Morpheus
11:03 You and Morpheus wrestle for pillow
11:15 Realize you're in wrong apartment

AFTERNOON

12:01 Get rocked to sleep
12:02 By stone throwing mob
2:37 Roll over
2:38 A CD account
5:45 Catch forty winks
5:46 From forty construction workers

EARLY EVENING

7:07 Hit the hay
7:08 Hay hits you back
8:59 Sweet dreams
9:00 Sour dreams
10:01 Sweet-and-sour dreams
10:37 Get a little shuteye
10:41 Using Krazy Glue

LATE EVENING

11:30 Turn on Johnny Carson
11:31 Ed gets jealous
1:28 Bout with insomnia
1:29 On the Sports Channel
4:34 Count sheep
5:34 In base seven
6:07 Dream the Impossible Dream
6:10 Change the wet sheets

SPECIAL BONUS!

The following sleeping positions are absolutely guaranteed to put you in a comatose state (not unlike Nebraska).

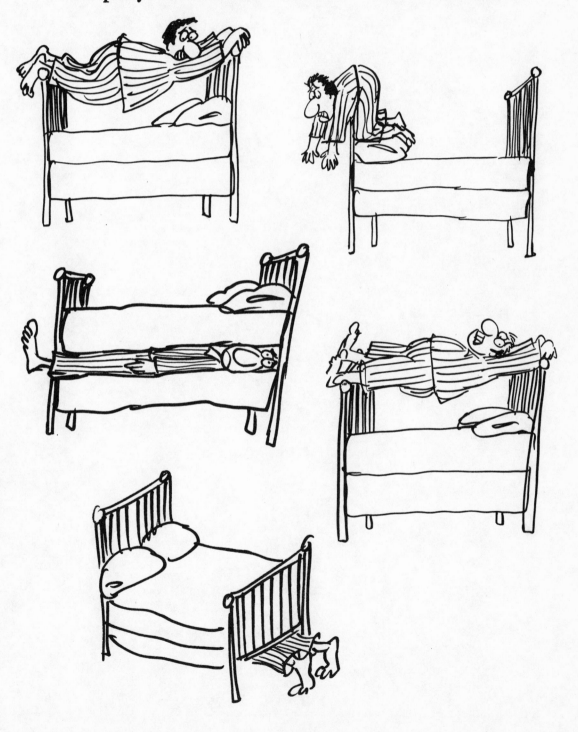

31. EARNING YOUR D.D. (DOCTORATE OF DEPRESSION)

Over the last thirty chapters, how far have you actually retrogressed?

That's the question you should be asking yourself because, right now, all you have are your feelings of worthlessness and despair, doom and desperation, as if your entire universe had suddenly become Pittsburgh.

Well, that's no cause for celebration. Who says you can maintain that great feeling? Just because your life is the "Pitts" today is no sure guarantee that you won't wake up tomorrow with some positive sense of self-realization.

Now, that can be a disturbing thought to just about any unsound mind.

Luckily, you don't have to live with that kind of sword over your head. For this final examination can determine, once and for all, whether you'll be spending the rest of your days in the arms of Brooke Shields, or in the arms of the law. To put it quite plainly, the lower you've sunk, the higher your score.

It's really that simple. After the exam, final downgrading will appear.

ANSWER THE QUESTIONS BELOW!

1. **He finds pleasure in being abused or dominated. He is a: _____.**
   a) Philistine
   b) Chauvinist
   c) Sadist
   d) Guest on David Letterman

2. **Who became morose over an assertion that he resembled David Eisenhower?**
   a) Octavius Frivolous
   b) Laconic the Elder
   c) Wince Lumbago
   d) David Eisenhower

3. **In 1929, world unemployment equaled:**
   a) The number of people not working
   b) 119,345,727 (±5)
   c) All of Teddy Kennedy's children
   d) None of the above

4. **Elavil produces an irresistible urge to fondle:**
   a) Dan Rather
   b) Moussaka
   c) Armenians
   d) None of the above

5. Julie Android is:
a) A popular actress who's half woman and half computer
b) A Jewish American Princess who's half woman and half computer, and therefore will never go down
c) A binary star of stage and screen
d) Just another droid named Julie

6. Claustrophobia is defined as:
a) A terrible fear of enclosed places
b) A terrible fear of Claus Von Bulow
c) Both a & b
d) Neither a or b

7. Of the following, which cannot be induced by hypnosis?
a) Migraines
b) Shortness
c) Insomnia
d) Allergies

8. Ann Dromeda was...
a) The first illegal alien to be deported to Neptune
b) Wife of Alfie Centauri and mother of his children
c) A nebulous schoolteacher from Nebraska
d) None of the above

9. Can you identify the famous WW II drag queen turned Kamakazi pilot?
a) Charlton Heston
b) Winston Churchill
c) Chester A. Garfield
d) Flaming Teriyaki

10. Which headline actually appeared in the National Enema?
a) "Handwriting Expert Proves Bert Parks is Howard Hughes"
b) "Haldeman and Ehrlichman to Wed in June"
c) "How Expectant Mothers Threaten America's Survival"
d) "How the Color of Your Tongue Reveals Your Personality"

11. A seven foot zucchini grown by Seymour Mendez could:
a) Perform imitations of John Glenn
b) Write poetry
c) Sing "Ain't We Got Fun" in Gaelic
d) Drive a Pontiac and tickle the mayor of Detroit, simultaneously

12. In Norse mythology, "Looki Looki Lu" was defined as:
a) A wondrous miracle; or the act of passing a Lithuanian through a semiporous filter
b) An eternal torment given to writers who defile the name John Simon; inflammation of the semicolon
c) A strange occurrence; the feeling of waking up and running a fever, while also running in the Kentucky Derby.
d) Huh? (was that in the book?)

13. Apocalypse, Nu?
a) What Rabbi Milton Sharpstein is expected to say in the year 2000
b) A new film being written by Francis Ford Coppola and Mel Brooks
c) What Rabbi Milton Sharpstein is expected to say in the year 2001
d) C'mon. That wasn't in the book!

14. What is the hemorrhoid remedy most favored by Princeton undergraduates?
a) Lavoris
b) Preppie H.
c) Gleem
d) Guacamole

15. What was E. F. Glutton's famous quote?
a) "Life is an exercise in futility; but that's OK, we all need the exercise."
b) "If God had wanted man to fly, he would have given him confirmed reservations."
c) "It is never too late to invest in your financial insecurity."
d) "The history of the world is written in blood, maybe that's why our ancestors were so anemic."

16. The definition of "Safe" sex is:
a) Masturbating while wearing a condom
b) Masticating while wearing a condom
c) Intercourse while sliding into home base
d) Intercourse while in a locked bank vault

17. What was Selma Lovehandle best known for?
a) Donating her organs so that a Cornish hen might live
b) Worshipping a bust of John Travolta carved from halvah
c) Referring to a Milky Way bar as her little "sugar"
d) Curing real estate agents of "Herpes Duplex"

18. **Which one of the following astrological qualities is true?**
    a) Aquarians are often found at a new nite spot called "Club Foot"
    b) Virgos frequently commit suicide by boring themselves to death
    c) Leos make the best hostages
    d) Geminis always have split personalities, particularly when the check comes

19. **Any westerner can train to be a yogi by:**
    a) Serving as an ottoman at the Iranian embassy
    b) Achieving the unification of his body, mind and spirit with two coeds
    c) Playing an ax murderer aboard the Titanic in the film "A Night To Be Dismembered"
    d) Denying himself all nourishment for over twelve years in order to protest the high cost of human suffering, as well as the high cost of room service

20. **Which is a definite sign of paranoia?**
    a) A suspicion that leprechauns are stealing your pinwheel hat
    b) A fear that you're being pursued by men in plaid sports jackets
    c) A feeling that you're being mocked by Oldsmobile dealers
    d) A recurring dream in which your nude body is being criticized by an entire set of the Encyclopaedia Britannica

ANSWERS

1-d, 2-d, 3-a, 4-d, 5-d, 6-c, 7-b, 8-d (although she did live with Alfie Centauri for over 700 million light years, they never had any children) 9-d, 10-c, 11-b, 12-d, 13-b, 14-b, 15-c, 16-d, 17-c, 18-c, 19-a, 20-a

OK. EACH CORRECT ANSWER IS WORTH TEN (10) POINTS

CHECK THE FOLLOWING PAGE FOR FINAL DOWNGRADING!

SCORE	DEGREE	COMMENTS
160-200	D.D.— (DOCTORATE OF DEPRESSION)	Incredible! Superb The only way you could get your consciousness raised is with a tow truck. On the evolutionary scale, you rank somewhere between an insurance agent and a serious ear infection. You're wretched, abhorrent, vile and loathesome, but a good disco dancer!
120-159	M.A.— (MASTER OF ATROPHY)	Pretty good! You're so squeamish that you even faint at the sight of a phonograph getting a needle. What fills you with anxiety is the idea of brushing your tooth. Still, you enjoy the simple things in life, like watching Siamese twins going through a subway turnstile. All your life, people have had no regard for you. Even in the Ku Klux Klan, you were short-sheeted.
80-119	M.S.— (MASTER OF SEDATION)	Not so hot. There's a lot of hard work ahead—an awful lot! So what happened? You had all the disadvantages—a mommy who bronzed your baby shoes while you were still wearing them—but you just never lived up to your lack of potential. Get with it! There's nothing stopping you from becoming an end table, or getting a job with the phone company.

40-79	**B.A.— (BACHELOR OF ALIENATION)**	Excuses. Excuses. We've heard them all before and we'll hear them all again — especially from over-achievers like yourself. And don't bother to deny it. The facts speak loud and clear. To be quite blunt, the chances of your attaining the Nirvana of total withdrawal are remote indeed!
0-39	**B.S.— (BACHELOR OF SANITY)**	Psychopathic delusions of jubilance.Insanely chipper. The list of symptoms goes on and on. We tried. But very little has been proven effective against those afflicted by true character and initiative. You have the emotional fiber and the intellectual stamina to reach the loftiest heights of personal satisfaction in every aspect of your life. Pity.

(No, you're not through yet. Turn the page for a final depressing thought...)

THE BEST YEARS OF YOUR LIFE
ARE STILL BEHIND YOU!

ABOUT THE AUTHOR

Born out of gridlock, in the backseat of a taxicab, Mr. Rudnitsky shares his birthdate with such notables as Helen Keller and Attila the Hun, which explains why so many of his contemporaries consider him a deaf-mute barbarian.

During his early years, his mother diligently attended to the household and, by age 22, he no longer needed to be breast-fed and was allowed to venture anywhere, as long as it didn't involve crossing the street.

Mr. Rudnitsky (that's Rud-Niet-Sky, Russian for "condominium") epitomizes the life-style he preaches, having received his Doctorate in Circular Reasoning from Columbia University. Over the past years, he has found more than enough time to co-author a number of books, including "1001 Ways You Reveal Your Personality," "1001 More Ways You Reveal Your Personality," "Love Codes," "How To Multiply Without Dividing" and, his latest, "Men Who Hate Themselves (And The Women Who Agree With Them)."

The New York Times has called his work "an intriguing series of semicolons...of special interest to tap dancers and amoebas."

A popular figure at seminars and lectures, Mr. Rudnitsky's sense of humor has been known to provoke audiences to near- riotous states of absence. Even at family gatherings, relatives often force him to dodge questions, and occasionally a few bricks.

For seventeen years, Mr. Rudnitsky has been a Creative Director at one of New York's most prestigious advertising agencies, and he soon expects to get his first paycheck. His numerous hobbies include imitating parsley and mating chickpeas. Mr. Rudnitsky died shortly before writing this book.

ABOUT THE ILLUSTRATOR

Jack Medoff illustrated the best-selling books, "Winning Through Intimidation" and "Looking Out For #1." His work has also appeared in many national magazines and newspapers, as well as his baby son's bedroom.

He lives a quiet life in Connecticut with his wife, son and Guinea Pig.